D1826041

'This book is an invitation to reflect deeply on the role of Mary in the mystery of our salvation. It is thorough, thoughtful, well researched and speaks to both heart and mind, for Mary is held in love by every disciple. Its reflection on the 'yes' of Mary is a key to understanding how she leads us, constantly, in our life of faith. Congratulations to Fr Martin Onuoha!'
– Vincent Cardinal Nichols, Cardinal, Archbishop of Westminster and President of the Catholic Bishops' Conference of England and Wales.

'Fr. Onuoha helps us understand how central Mary is to the theological vision of Joseph Ratzinger. This is a vision that is Christocentric, liturgical, and contemplative with Mary as the supreme model for all the faithful - men as well as women.'
– Robert Fastiggi, Ph.D., Bishop Kevin M. Britt Chair of Dogmatic Theology and Christology, Sacred Heart Major Seminary, Detroit, Michigan USA.

'Fr Onuoha's presentation of the Marian mystery in the theology of Joseph Ratzinger and its significance for the resolution of the ecclesial crisis of our era is likely to become a classic work in the fields of Mariology, ecclesiology and Ratzinger studies.'
– Professor Tracey Rowland, St. John Paul II Chair of Theology, University of Notre Dame (Australia); a member of the International Theological Commission, and a member of the editorial board of the English language edition of Communio (co-founded by Ratzinger) and winner of the 2020 Ratzinger Price.

'I welcome here a significant voice to Ratzinger studies and to the Marian renewal of the Church in accord with the vision of *Lumen Gentium*.'
– Professor Matthew Levering, James N. and Mary D. Perry Jr. Chair of Theology at Mundelein Seminary, and Co-Director of the Chicago Theological Initiative.

'I have known Dr Onuoha since 2006. I have supervised both his Master's and Doctoral theses. I am not surprised that he is doing a significant work in the academic context. Doctor Onuoha not only masters profoundly Joseph Ratzinger's thought, but also draws from it broad conclusions to illuminate different areas of theology, history and law. His book is certainly worthwhile.'

– Prof. Antonio Ducay, Professor of Systematic Theology, Pontifical University of the Holy Cross Rome, Italy.

'Rev. Fr. Martin Onuoha offers in this thoughtful and thought-provoking work a serious and comprehensive exposition of the theology of Joseph Ratzinger. Well researched, captivating in content and beautifully written, this book represents an important and rich contribution to Mariology and Ecclesiology.'

– +Lucius Iwejuru Ugorji, Bishop of Umuahia and Apostolic Administrator of Ahiara Diocese.

'With the sources in one place Fr Onuoha's work provides a welcome opportunity to return anew to Ratzinger's ecclesiology through the Marian lens. This Marian lens opens fresh perspectives on Ratzinger's thought on the Church and insights to his overall opus.'

– Dr. Frances McKenna, author of 'Innovation within Tradition: Joseph Ratzinger and Reading the Women of Scripture'.

ACTIO DIVINA

ACTIO DIVINA

The Marian Mystery of the Church in the Theology of Joseph Ratzinger (Benedict XVI)

Martin Ifeanyi Onuoha

Peter Lang

Oxford • Bern • Berlin • Bruxelles • New York • Wien

Bibliographic information published by Die Deutsche Nationalbibliothek.
Die Deutsche Nationalbibliothek lists this publication in the Deutsche Nationalbibliografie;
detailed bibliographic data is available on the Internet at http://dnb.d-nb.de.

A catalogue record for this book is available from the British Library.

Library of Congress Cataloging-in-Publication Data

Names: Onuoha, Martin Ifeanyi, 1973- author.
Title: Actio divina : the Marian mystery of the church in the theology of
  Joseph Ratzinger (Benedict XVI) / Martin Ifeanyi Onuoha.
Description: Oxford ; New York : Peter Lang, 2022. | Includes
  bibliographical references and index.
Identifiers: LCCN 2021039668 (print) | LCCN 2021039669 (ebook) | ISBN
  9781800793972 (paperback) | ISBN 9781800793989 (ebook) | ISBN
  9781800793996 (epub)
Subjects: LCSH: Mary, Blessed Virgin, Saint--History of doctrines--21st
  century. | Church--History of doctrines--21st century. | Catholic
  Church--Doctrines.--History--20th century. | Catholic
  Church--Doctrines--History--21st century. | Benedict XVI, Pope, 1927-
Classification: LCC BT610 .O575 2022 (print) | LCC BT610 (ebook) | DDC
  232.91--dc23
LC record available at https://lccn.loc.gov/2021039668
LC ebook record available at https://lccn.loc.gov/2021039669

Cover design by Brian Melville for Peter Lang.
Photograph by Martin Ifeanyi Onuoha.

ISBN   978-1-80079-397-2 (print)
ISBN   978-1-80079-398-9 (ePDF)
ISBN   978-1-80079-399-6 (ePub)
© Peter Lang Group AG 2022

Published by Peter Lang Ltd, International Academic Publishers,
52 St Giles, Oxford, OX1 3LU, United Kingdom
oxford@peterlang.com, www.peterlang.com

This publication has been peer reviewed.

In gratitude to the Eucharistic Heart of Jesus and the Immaculate Heart of Mary on the 20th Anniversary of my priestly ordination

Contents

Foreword 1   ix

Foreword 2   xvii

Preface   xxi

Acknowledgements   xxv

List of Abbreviations   xxvii

PART I   1

CHAPTER 1
The Church's Self-Understanding   3

PART II   11

CHAPTER 2
Resurgence of Ecclesiotypical Mariology   13

CHAPTER 3
Main Ecclesiological Models of Vatican II   29

PART III   43

CHAPTER 4
Ratzinger on the Marian Nature of the Church   45

CHAPTER 5
The Liturgy: Ecclesial Self-Expression as Marian Mystery   63

CHAPTER 6
The Marian Church: Mission and Ministry   91

Bibliography   105

Index   117

Foreword 1

Martin Ifeanyi Onuoha's two books on the Marian thought of Joseph Ratzinger – the one you hold in your hands, and its 'prologue', *Mary, Daughter Zion: An Introduction to the Mariology of Joseph Ratzinger* – are an extended commentary not only on the whole corpus of Ratzinger but also, in a different way, on the Catholic Church of the past sixty years. In these decades, in Western societies, many people have left the Church entirely or else have found themselves so interiorly alienated from the Church that there is little chance their children will remain in the Church. The result has been an accelerating apostasy. People today believe in the Gospel less, participate in the Eucharistic liturgy less, pray to God less, receive the other sacraments less and so on – the very opposite of Vatican II's hopes.

Theologically, the marks of the crisis are twofold. First, within the Church, a significant group of laity and clergy, not only in Ratzinger's native Germany but all over the world, seek to redefine Catholicism into something that would be unrecognizable to previous generations. There is a movement to rupture Catholicism from its past, getting rid of many of the Church's moral teachings and many matters pertaining to the Church's solemn understanding of the sacraments. This movement understands itself to be either an open dogmatic rupture, or an enlightened discovery that the dogmatic teachings of the second millennium were never really binding dogma. In either case, it is not hard to see that the proposed changes would strip the ground from every element of Catholic doctrine; there would no longer be a reason to be a Catholic rather than a Protestant, and no pope or Council could ever teach in an authoritative or binding manner again. In fact, the pope or Council that taught these ruptures would thereby be revealed as lacking in authority to teach. All too often, one hears that it is the 'Spirit' who justifies such changes, but the doctrine of the Spirit was itself solemnly formulated by a Council and was contested by many in the fourth century. There is no logical reason that the dogmatic understanding of the Spirit should stand while other dogmatic teachings fall.

The goal of this rupture-movement within the Church is clear: to assimilate fully into contemporary Western culture, in which the sexual revolution and certain economic and political outlooks govern acceptable thinking. The actual teachings of the Gospel fade away, while what remain are certain liberative stances taken by Jesus – not the liberation from slavery to sin and death that he actually brought, but rather a liberation from Jewish cult and Roman empire (reflective not of the actual Jesus but of modernity's theopolitical dreams).

Second, unfortunately, another rupture-movement has emerged. This movement, like the above one, began already in the immediate aftermath (or, in certain ways, during) the Second Vatican Council. It finds the Council's documents to be deeply problematic. In this regard, it is similar to the religiously liberal movement, which also has little use for the letter of the Council's documents. For both movements, the Council functions at best as a pastoral Council, but one whose pastoral recommendations almost immediately became outdated. For this self-styled 'traditionalist' movement, *Sacrosanctum Concilium* and *Gaudium et Spes* are deeply troubling, and even central elements of *Dei Verbum* and *Lumen Gentium* come under suspicion. Documents such as *Dignitatis Humanae* and *Nostra Aetate* are more firmly rejected as mistaken and in need of being jettisoned. In various writings, Ratzinger responded both to the traditionalist movement and to the religiously liberal movement. He argued at length that both of them were dead ends, although he well understood the problems that have encouraged the rise of both movements.[1]

In this context, Onuoha's profound reading of Ratzinger's Marian theology invites two thoughts, or, more precisely, two hopes. One is that it may well be the Second Vatican Council's teachings on the *Blessed Virgin Mary* – teachings promoted by Ratzinger, Pope John Paul II, and others – that provide the impulse for the renewal sought by the Council, a renewal

---

[1]   See also the essays in M. L. Lamb and M. Levering (eds), *Vatican II: Renewal within Tradition* (Oxford: Oxford University Press, 2008); and M. L. Lamb and M. Levering (eds), *The Reception of Vatican II* (Oxford: Oxford University Press, 2017).

that is now more urgently needed than ever. A second is that it may well be *African pastors and theologians* who ultimately enable the Church to overcome the extremes of religious liberalism and reactionary traditionalism.

Onuoha highlights Ratzinger's and the Council's insistence on Mary as the type of the Church. Specifically, Onuoha judges that 'Ratzinger's Mariological and Ecclesial thinking (the two are always linked in his understanding) is a crucial resource for the recovery and the renewal of basic teachings which feed the hearts as well as the minds of believers'. Among these basic teachings, Onuoha includes the priority of the *Logos*, the Marian fiat or self-surrender in love, the Church's feminine receptivity (not merely passive but also active) to the Word of God, the essential historical veracity of the New Testament, the universality of redemptive grace, the value of virginity, the importance of contemplation and interiority over against mere 'activism', the priority of being over doing, the complementarity of man and woman, the Church as a communion of persons rather than merely a bureaucratic institution, the need for *kenotic* humility in the face of truth and the nature of 'rational worship' (Rom 12:1). For Onuoha and Ratzinger, the Council's decision to include the treatment of Mary *within* the Dogmatic Constitution on the Church, *Lumen Gentium*, is decisive. In thinking about the Church, we must reflect upon these above foundational 'Marian' principles, because the renewal of the Church will come about through a reassertion of these principles. The turning (or re-turning) of human beings towards Christ will take a Marian form – one that stands apart from the anthropocentric 'activism' of our day, and is open afresh to the inner mystery of God's presence in the incarnate Lord.

Lumen Gentium teaches, 'Having entered deeply into the history of salvation, Mary, in a way, unites in her person and re-echoes the most important doctrines of the faith: and when she is the subject of preaching and worship she prompts the faithful to come to her Son, to his sacrifice and to the love of the Father.'[2] This is the very lesson that Onuoha draws out of Ratzinger: the Church learns how to be the Church by meditation

2   LG 65.

upon Mary. As *Lumen Gentium* further explains, 'Devoutly meditating on her and contemplating her in the light of the Word made man, the Church reverently penetrates more deeply into the great mystery of the Incarnation and becomes more and more like her spouse.'[3] A Church that neglects Mary will struggle to be configured to Christ, since it will lose touch with the Marian attributes that are crucial for being open to her Son by his Spirit. A Church that recalls Mary – not as a mere individual but as a person who shows the Church how to follow her Son – will be, to that degree, a healthy Church. In this regard *Lumen Gentium* reports, 'As St. Ambrose taught, the Mother of God is a type of the Church in the order of faith, charity, and perfect union with Christ.'[4]

As Ratzinger and Onuoha remark, the current crisis in the Church and world has a variety of dimensions, including loss of faith in God the Creator, loss of liturgical symbolism and the sense of mystery, historical-critical doubts about whether the Gospels accurately teach about the person of Jesus, loss of a sense of sin and so on. Catholic scholars have proposed various solutions, such as improved catechesis, reinvigorated theology and a renewed liturgy. But I am struck by the thought that Onuoha – drawing upon Ratzinger and *Lumen Gentium* – has arrived at the heart of the matter. Namely, what we learn from Onuoha is that for Christian faith to be renewed, the Church's Marian identity must first be recovered, so that the Church is able to be fully open, in self-surrendering love, to the incarnate Son of God.

In this recovery, furthermore, it seems that African pastors and theologians may lead the way. Indeed, Onuoha's reflections remind me of Robert Cardinal Sarah's, even though Cardinal Sarah does not say very much about Mary (nor does Onuoha mention Sarah). In *God or Nothing*, Cardinal Sarah recalls his formation in Christian faith: 'My father taught me great love for the Virgin Mary. I can still see him kneel down on the sand of Ourous to pray the Angelus every day at noon and in the evening. I never forgot those moments when he closed his eyes to give thanks to Mary. I imitated

---

3   LG 65.
4   LG 63, citing St Ambrose, *Commentary on Luke* 2.7, PL 15, 1555.

him and recited my prayers to the Mother of Jesus at his side.'[5] Cardinal Sarah, like Ratzinger, is a profoundly Christocentric theologian; and for him, too, the holy Mass is the very centre of life. Sarah recognizes the centrality of configuration to Christ so as to be 'a man who is crucified with Christ'.[6] He also draws from Pope John Paul II the lesson that 'the priestly vocation is inseparable from the Virgin Mary …. The life of a priest is inconceivable without a filial bond with Mary'.[7]

Like Ratzinger and Onuoha, Cardinal Sarah perceives an intensifying crisis in the world and in the Church. He states, 'I think that the immense economic, military, technological, and media influence of a godless West could be a disaster for the world. If the West does not convert to Christ, it could end up making the whole world pagan.'[8] For Sarah, the pre-conciliar West is represented by the priests who gave their lives for the conversion of Africa; whereas the post-conciliar West is spiritually adrift, reaping the bitter fruit of Enlightenment rejection of God and Christ. As he asks with great sorrow, 'How can we Africans comprehend the fact that Europeans no longer believe what they gave us so joyfully, in the worst possible conditions?'[9] Sarah addresses hedonism, materialism, the sexual revolution, gender theory, pornography's distortion of sexuality, 'the powerful European and American sex industry', homosexual 'marriage', abortion advocacy, the contraception industry and so on.[10] He notes that the enlightened thinking of the West is now atheistic. He observes that 'most Western populations now regard Jesus as a sort of idea but not as an event, much less as a person whom the apostles and many witnesses of the Gospel met and loved and to whom they consecrated their whole life'.[11]

This atheistic attitude, he notes, is not the result of an inexorable march of reason, but rather is a choice about how to live. Put simply, the

---

5   R. Sarah with N. Diat, *God or Nothing: A Conversation on Faith*, trans. M. J. Miller (San Francisco, CA: Ignatius Press, 2015), 165.

6   Ibid., 127.

7   Ibid., 128.

8   Ibid., 146.

9   Ibid., 148.

10   Ibid., 158.

11   Ibid., 167.

majority of cultures in the West do not wish to know God. Cardinal Sarah surmises that the reason is the desire for self-sufficiency – a demand for self-creation, for full dominance over nature. The result is not happiness but a tragic 'spiritual destitution' and meaninglessness, due to the absence of 'the things of eternity'.[12] Cardinal Sarah warns in the starkest terms: 'The man who ignores God and turns his own instincts into godlike standards for all things is headed for destruction. Today we are confronted with one of the last stages of the civilization of diversion. The alternative is simple: if mankind reforms itself, it will live, but if its headlong flight persists, civilization will become a hell.'[13]

Some African theologians today are pulled towards forms of liberation theology, in which economic and political programs take centre stage. In such theologies, sanctification and Christian mission are conceived primarily in terms of a fight against systemic structures of sin so as to build more just economic and political institutions and societies.[14] In the midst

12   Ibid., 189.
13   Ibid., 193.
14   See for example Jean-Marc Ela's misleading, but widely shared, claim about 'the nature of faith as key to the discovery of the human being and the world as a task to realize day by day until human beings have been brought to the perfect stature of all things in Jesus Christ. After all, what animates a Christian's faith is the perception of an unfinished world placed in our hands by God. In a sense, the world is not to be saved, but reinvented – or, if one prefers, made over by the power of the gospel. Faith impels us to toil in order that all reality become, in Jesus Christ, a new creation. A concern to inscribe in the here and now, in the present moment of human beings and their history, the signs of a world to come, is what gives the faith of Christians its thrust. Faith in the God of hope endows men and women with the energy that mobilizes them to ready the new morning of a new creation, in which they will at last be invested with their dignity. The person of faith is a person of creation. His or her mission in the world is to build a dis-alienated society, a society in which all women and men find it possible to really live' (J.-M. Ela, *African Cry*, trans. R. R. Barr [Maryknoll, NY: Orbis, 1986], 92–93). Ela has misidentified the Christian mission in the world. Christians are not separatists aloof from economic and political matters, but neither is the *focus* of Christianity rightly upon building a better social order. Ela's perspective is not novel but rather reflects religious liberalism's effort to reinvent Christianity: see Ernst Troeltsch's 1910 essay, 'On the Possibility of a Liberal Christianity', in Troeltsch, *Religion in History*, trans. J. L. Adams and W. F. Bense (Minneapolis, MN: Fortress, 1991), 343–359.

of grave injustice – both in Africa *and* in the West, as Sarah ceaselessly points out – Christians must stand up against evildoing, including unjust leaders and unjust structures that poison society. Nevertheless, Christians must remain focused upon God and his *present* reign in Christ, a reign that demands that we suffer in self-sacrificial love and that we proclaim our hope regarding Christ's coming in glory to bring about the fullness of deified life. In our earthly pilgrimage, the source and summit of Catholic life is the worship of the triune God through participating liturgically in Christ's Pasch, by which Christ conquers sin and death and elevates believers into the life of the Trinity.

It can easily happen that supposedly liberative economic and political programs fail to achieve the hoped-for results. Cardinal Sarah experienced the impact of Marxist claims about the class struggle in his home country of Guinea. In Guinea, 'the myth of equality resulted in a bloody dictatorship', and Sarah draws the conclusion that 'God willed that human beings should be complementary so as to aid and support one another mutually'.[15] The centre of the Church's attention must always be turned to God, to 'personal contact with Jesus'.[16] This contact with the Lord sustains true political witness, but its fundamental purpose is to be united to the Lord, not to deliver political benefits. Without God's love, without self-renunciation in love for God, nothing is enough. Politically, Sarah believes that 'in a human society, a Christian will always be more or less a dissident'.[17] The truly human solution must be to reject the notion of life as 'a feast without God' and to return to contemplation and the 'interior life', striving 'to agree with the Father's will and to correspond to it'.[18] A more Marian proposal could hardly be found!

---

15   R. Sarah, *God or Nothing*, 190.

16   Ibid., 145.

17   R. Sarah with N. Diat, *The Day Is Now Far Spent*, trans. M. J. Miller (San Francisco, CA: Ignatius Press, 2019), 293.

18   Ibid., 250–251, 225. He comments: 'Do priests busy themselves with Christ and the evangelization of the world or with the earthly well-being of men? The supernatural seems to be absorbed and engulfed in the natural …. We no longer see heaven, and we no longer see God, either' (ibid., 49).

Although Cardinal Sarah generally says little about Mary, he recognizes that Mary is the model of the receptive and contemplative Church who can truly receive the Word of God. In *The Power of Silence*, Sarah depicts Mary as 'entirely absorbed by contemplation, adoration, and prayer', and he suggests that it is for this reason that Mary pre-eminently, among all humans, does 'the great works of God'.[19] Along the same lines, he maintains: 'The attitude of Mary is that of listening. She is completely turned to the word of the Son …. Her *fiat* is total and joyful. She intends to receive God's will through Jesus.'[20] Thus to understand the Church, the Bride of Christ, we must look to Mary.

As readers will discover, Onuoha's project goes beyond Cardinal Sarah's and in certain ways completes it. Onuoha shows us, first and foremost, how Marian the theology of Joseph Ratzinger is. He gives us a new way of reading Ratzinger. This in itself is no small accomplishment. Second, he gives us a new possibility for thinking about the Church and its renewal. *Lumen Gentium* turns out to hold the key: to renew the Church, we will need to renew the Church's Marian elements in all their dimensions. Third, he shows us that it may well be African Catholic theology that will lead the way. African Catholicism has the necessary grounding in worship, desire for salvation from sin and death, yearning for the transcendent God and understanding of human nature. In saying this, I am not being nostalgic about the situations of the countries of Africa. I am simply taking notice of where the spiritual resources are and paying attention to what is before our eyes. I welcome here a significant voice to Ratzinger studies and to the Marian renewal of the Church in accord with the vision of *Lumen Gentium*.

Professor Matthew Levering
James N. and Mary D. Perry Jr Chair of Theology at Mundelein
Seminary
Co-Director of the Chicago Theological Initiative

19   R. Sarah with N. Diat, *The Power of Silence: Against the Dictatorship of Noise*, trans. M. J. Miller (San Francisco, CA: Ignatius Press, 2017), 113.
20   Ibid., 115.

Foreword 2

Actio Divina: The Marian Mystery of the Church in the Theology of Joseph Ratzinger (Benedict XVI) is not merely an account of the nexus between Mariology and ecclesiology in the thought of Joseph Ratzinger, but it is also a pathology report on the health, or rather sickness of the being of the Church, at a time when the Marian mystery has in many places been occluded.

The need for the Marian mystery was earlier emphasized by Hans Urs von Balthasar, one of Ratzinger's intellectual heroes and *Communio* journal co-founder and collaborator. In his *Elucidations*, Balthasar observed:

> Since the Council the Church has to a large extent put off its mystical characteristics; it has become a Church of permanent conversations, organizations, advisory commissions, congresses, synods, commissions, academies, parties, pressure groups, functions, structures and restructurings, sociological experiments, statistics: that is to say, more than ever a male Church, if perhaps one should not say a sexless entity, in which woman may gain for herself a place to the extent that she is ready herself to become such an entity. (p. 70)

Balthasar concluded that 'the masses run away from such a Church'. Such a Church is no longer the Church militant, a community of pilgrims fighting spiritual battles against the enemies of Christ while on the road to their eternal home, but simply, a 'photocopying church'. Similarly, Cardinal Julius Dopfner famously remarked 'the Church of the post-conciliar period is a huge construction site ... where the blueprint has been lost and everyone continues to build according to his taste'.

In the present work, Fr Onuoha notes that 'the link between Mary and the Church prevents a false model of 'renewal' of a quasi-political or corporatist kind' such as Balthasar described above, and it 're-establishes the balance between male and female forms of being within the Church'. Quite simply a Marian understanding of the Church as a bride and a mother, is a radically different understanding from that of a corporation or other bureaucratic institution. It has been said of the late Fr Benedict Groeschel, the founder of the Franciscan Friars of the Renewal, that he referred to the corporate dimension of the contemporary Church as the 'hippopotamus' and would joke to his friends that they should steer clear of the hippopotamus.

In a speech to the Congregation for Bishops, Pope Francis said that bishops are not chief executive officers of a business enterprise. They are not corporate executives. They need to be evangelists and men of prayer and spiritual strength. They need to be accessible to the laity. In an earlier and perhaps more famous address he said that clergy need to smell like their sheep. Leaving aside the folksy metaphor (that was the subject of some mirth is parts of the world where there are a lot of badly smelling four-legged sheep) his meaning was that clerics should actually know those under their pastoral care and spend time with them. Bishops and priests should be in a relationship with their people that is *personal*, not what sociologists would call *rational-bureaucratic*.

Joseph Ratzinger/Benedict XVI is of one-mind with Pope Francis in holding a negative judgment on the corporate model of the Church. In his book *Called to Communion,* Ratzinger wrote: 'The more administrative machinery we construct, be it the most modern, the less place there is for the Spirit, the less place there is for the Lord, and the less freedom there is.' He added that in his opinion, 'we ought to begin an unsparing examination of conscience on this point at all levels in the Church'. As Fr. Onuoha observes: 'Joseph Ratzinger fights "tooth and nail" the vision of the Church as a structure or programme for action.'

This work by Fr Onuoha is therefore highly valuable at this moment in the life of the Church. It not only provides us with a window into the ecclesiology and Mariology of Joseph Ratzinger, but it provides an outline of the theological solution to the problem of the hippopotamus. Quite simply, many have lost an understanding of the Marian mystery of the Church and this needs to be restored. The Church is not an 'it' but a 'she'. The solutions to the problems of the Church are theological and spiritual not sociological. As a mother the Church's fruitfulness depends on something outside of herself, specifically, fidelity to Christ and the reception of the Word communicated liturgically. Take away this spousal and maternal understanding of the Church and one is on the slippery slope to a utilitarian vision of the Church as merely another multinational corporation with an interest in philanthropy.

As Ratzinger recognized, any worldview in which little or no recognition is given to the metaphysical will overlook the mystery aspect of the Church and we are living through a very anti-metaphysical cycle in Western intellectual life. Fr Onuoha is not however one of those blind to the dimensions of metaphysics and mystery. In one of my favourite passages of this account of the Marian mystery he writes:

> The *Logos*, the Person of Christ, cannot be historicized to the point of limitlessness. He is not just Jesus of Nazareth, shut up within the confines of his direct and immediate place, words and actions in time. He is truly God the Son, the Incarnate Word of God, at once human and divine, historical, and yet beyond history. The particular and the universal, known to Greek philosophy as the One and the Many, are not in any conflict with Him. Rather, in and through Him, is realized the healing of the rupture in that primordial link. Christ is both one and many, Alpha and Omega, within sequence and beyond all sequence, truly *Logos Incarnatus*. (pp. 38–39)

The *Logos Incarnatus* is made present on the altars of the world in the sacrament of the Eucharist and thus Eucharistic theology is intrinsically linked to both ecclesiology and Mariology. In Christ, God Himself becomes bodily human existence. In Christ, God Himself has fostered that fusion with humanity, so that the people of God can enter into connection with Him to form a single spiritual body. For this reason, it can be said that the Eucharist makes the Church. The Church, however, could not be, without the immaculate grace of Mary's conception and consent to the Incarnation.

Fr Onuoha's presentation of the Marian mystery in the theology of Joseph Ratzinger and its significance for the resolution of the ecclesial crisis of our era is likely to become a classic work in the fields of Mariology, ecclesiology and Ratzinger studies.

Professor Tracey Rowland
St. John Paul II Chair of Theology, University of Notre Dame
(Australia)

Preface

In our first volume – *Mary, Daughter Zion*[1] – I tried to show how the Mariology of Joseph Ratzinger (Pope Emeritus Benedict XVI), though formally fragmented, is nevertheless a cohering and coherent body of thought. Everything proceeds, as he insists repeatedly, from a proper understanding of the character and effects of Mary's unconditional consent to the Will of God upon which the Incarnation depends and which is, also, the conception of the Church. She is not the focus of some optional devotion within the life of the Church; she is the mother of its life. Her inclusion therefore within a document about the Church at the Second Vatican Council is not a relegation of the importance that she has always had in Catholic thinking and devotion, but a reassertion of her centrality in the Church's life and especially of its self-understanding. For the Church is not its own body, but Christ's body born of Mary. The Church is founded upon the life of a person received through the consent of a person.

This is not new teaching. It is based solidly on a close and sustained reading of the Scriptures and Patristic theology, but Ratzinger gives it new force and depth, and he addresses it directly to a world which he sees as increasingly likely to have lost the power to understand it. In this way, his theology vindicates H. M. Marron's contention that 'the newest pages of our theology are often very ancient pages which have been found again in their original freshness and lasting value only after long and arduous search.'[2] Here, Ratzinger is not a voice in the wilderness. He has found listeners within and without the Church.

Ratzinger's Marian theology is especially important at the present time, some fifty-six years after Vatican II. The Council was followed, as he has ruefully observed, not by the hoped-for renewal but by divisions and much apparent decline in many of its established modes of life. Some

---

1   M. Onuoha, *Mary, Daughter Zion: An Introduction to the Mariology of Joseph Ratzinger (Benedict XVI)*, (Oxford: Peter Lang Ltd, International Academic Publishers, 2021).

2   H. M. Marron, *Time and Timeliness* (New York: Sheed and Ward, 1969), 10.

have blamed this on timidity – a refusal to liberalize Church doctrine and practice in accordance with 'the Spirit of the Council'. Others have blamed the Council itself for authorizing a flexibility which undermined Catholic teaching, identity and self-confidence. The role of Mary in salvation history and in the active liturgical and devotional life of the Church was, as it were, rather put to one side in this period, though, as we have seen, Paul VI's *Marialis Cultus*, the deep devotion of St John Paul II to the Mother of God (*Totus Tuus*) and Ratzinger's carefully developed thought ensured that it was not wholly forgotten.

Ratzinger's contribution is especially important in that he has displaced entirely the perspectives of those who see the Council as either a welcome or unwelcome rupture in the history of the Church. He reads its documents and ponders them with the same attention that he gives to reading the Scriptures and the Fathers.

I want now to show how Ratzinger offers a whole new dimension, not only to Mariology, but also to theology itself. He finds new things there but no rupture rather, to use his famous phrase, a 'hermeneutic of continuity'(though, more recently, he uses the phrase 'hermeneutic of reform'; the two words – 'continuity' and 'reform' – belong together in his view).[3] The Council, he thinks, gave fresh impetus to the understanding of the Church and of Mary and, more importantly, to the living connection between the two. Nothing was lost here, everything gained.

Ratzinger's stance here has something of a prophetic character. He writes to the world now and to its immediate future. He sees a Church beset by internal problems and the indifference or scorn of the wider world. He

3   On the reception and application of Vatican II, later, as Benedict XVI, he says: 'On the one hand, there is an interpretation that I would call "a hermeneutic of discontinuity and rupture"; it has frequently availed itself of the sympathies of the mass media, and also one trend of modern theology. On the other, there is the "hermeneutic of reform", of renewal in the continuity of the one subject-Church which the Lord has given to us. She is a subject which increases in time and develops, yet always remaining the same, the one subject of the journeying People of God.' Pope Benedict XVI, *Address to the Roman Curia Offering Them His Christmas Greetings* Thursday (22 December 2005), in: <http://www.vatican.va/content/benedict-xvi/en/speeches/2005/december/documents/hf_ben_xvi_spe_2005122 2_roman-curia.html> (Accessed: 30 November 2021).

foresees further divisions and a shrinkage of scale and influence, but he is not a doom-monger. The Church is God's life and action (*actio divina*) in the world and for the world, it was conceived through the immaculate grace of Mary's conception and consent, but it needs to understand this if it is to fulfil God's salvific purposes. The Church should rejoice in its present weakness because in that weakness lies the strength that comes from Mary's consent to be governed by God's life in her and by nothing else whatsoever.

In this way, Ratzinger speaks to our times. He does not talk about the Council as a past event or as a point of change but, through its documents and only in those, as a guide to present understanding whose force has still not been fully received. For example, in the light of the Council, he advocates a re-reading of the four Marian dogmas in ecclesial context as manifest fruits in the liturgy and life of the church from typologically discernible seeds.[4] The link between Mary and the Church is crucial to this appreciation of the Council. It prevents a false model of 'renewal' of a quasi-political or corporatist kind, it is nourished by the Scriptures and Patristic theology, it is a remedy for false models of liturgical life, it re-establishes the balance between male and female forms of being within the Church and it could and should ground a proper ecumenism.

Mariology, understood in this way, is not at the margins of religion, or of thought and reality in general, but at the centre. Mary, in and through Christ, reveals the inner truth of being, the truth about 'personhood', which is relationality, leading to the 'beautiful' unity that is the *finis* of worship, and is in itself ultimately worship.[5] The realization, 'on a deeper level', on the ontological level, of who man is, and what creation is meant to be, renders futile all divisions and resolves partisan and competition-motivated conflicts, in the realization of the innate unity in the *Logos*. What is said here of Mary applies also to the Church, since Mary is the Church, and the Church is Marian. Like Mary, she is a person, a 'yes', the manifestation of the beautiful truth of unity issuing from relationality.

---

4   Cf. J. Ratzinger and V. Messori, *The Ratzinger Report: An Exclusive Interview on the State of the Church* (San Francisco, CA: Ignatius Press, 1985), 107.

5   We have dealt with this in another volume – *Mary, Daughter Zion*, which led the foundation for this book.

Hence, Ratzinger justifiably upholds and defends the message of *Lumen Gentium* as a principal gateway to the resolution of the various crises that he diagnosed in our time (God crisis, Church crisis, crisis of woman, etc.). The decision to put the unity of Mary and the Church in one document, ending on the theme of holiness, is a call for a return to the one message of unity, of the Scriptures, of salvation history, the intrinsic unity of all reality – which is ultimately holiness. Ratzinger insists that the proper understanding of the Mary-Church reality represented by this document will reveal the Church's nature as a person, whose mirror and paradigm Mary is. The feminine, actively receptive visage, which is the true hermeneutics of the 'yes' of Mary, shows the Church, not only her nature, but also her proper demeanour in all aspects, always, but especially at this present difficult time. The fullness of the truth of this nature is realized in her living of the mystery of the *actio divina*, the liturgy, which, according to Ratzinger, is her constitution and defines her mission and ministry.

Acknowledgements

This book and its antecedent, *Mary, Daughter Zion: An Introduction to the Mariology of Joseph Ratzinger* were accepted by *Pontificia Università della Santa Croce, Rome*, for the award of a doctoral degree in 2013 under the tittle *The Mariology of Joseph Ratzinger: An Insight into the Church's Self-understanding*, and subsequently edited and printed for the university in 2014 and, in 2015, for use of seminarians in Nigeria, with the tittle, *Mary, Mother of the Church. The Church's Self-understanding in the Mariology of Ratzinger/Benedict XVI*. It is now further developed into two books that, I hope, could serve as valuable academic resources for theology, especially Marian, Ecclesiological and, more precisely, Ratzinger studies. The core arguments and a substantial part of the original are retained. The two books are intentionally left without conclusion. Consistent with Ratzinger's avowed intentions, they are intended to provide 'a spur to further thinking on these subjects'.[1] In his *Daughter Zion*, he set out, in his very words, 'merely to open the reader's eyes to the layer of meaning that can then make the approach to larger works possible'.[2] I can only wish I have in some ways aided that vital effort.

I earnestly thank God for the gift of life, health, inspiration and strength. I am also infinitely grateful to the Blessed Virgin for her maternal closeness and unfailing assistance. May I register, too, my indebtedness to *Pontificia Università della Santa Croce*, for offering me the wonderful opportunity that made this work possible, and to Professor Antonio Ducay and other professors and staff members.

1   J. Ratzinger, *Values in a Time of Upheaval* (San Francisco, CA: Ignatius Press, 2006), 8.
2   J. Ratzinger, *Daughter Zion: Meditations on the Church's Marian Belief* (San Francisco, CA: Ignatius Press, 1983), 7–8.

I pray for the repose of my late bishop, Rt. Rev. V. A. Chikwe, a formidable pillar of encouragement, and the late bishop Brian Noble who invited me to serve in the UK. Many thanks, too, to Bishop Mark Davies for his fatherly closeness and invaluable support. I am also extremely grateful to my parents, Nze D. O. Onuoha and the late Nneoha Celestina Onuoha, and my family for their love. I remember with immense affection and gratitude all my friends, benefactors and well-wishers. Deserving special mentions are the late Mr Albert Weber and George Kurtz (may they rest in the Lord's peace), Diane Kurtz, and the family, Mons. E. R. Walden, Mr/s Jim & Joanne Bell and Joe & Brenda Dugan. May the Lord also bless and reward Sr. Jo Bull, Padre John Franco and Padre Eugenio (RIP) for their invaluable support. I pray a special blessing on the parishioners of Our Lady and the Apostles, Shaw Heath, St Ambrose, Adswood, St Vincent's, Bramhall, Stockport; Holy Angels', Hale Barns; St Clare's and St Werburgh's, Chester; St Joseph's, Birkenhead; the members of the Nigerian African Chaplaincy, Liverpool; and the Maryvale Catholic Institute, Birmingham, United Kingdom, where I have served all these years.

The humbling affability and generous gesture of His Eminence, Cardinal Vincent Nichols; Bishop Lucius Ugorji; and Professors Robert Fastiggi, Tracey Rowland, Matthew Levering, Emmanuel Nworu and Bernard Beatty in being so obliging to carefully read these manuscripts and provide Forewords, blurbs and corrections/suggestions for the publication are indeed priceless.

Abbreviations

AAS	*Acta Apostolicae Sedis*
AG	Second Vatican Council, *Ad Gentes*, Decree on the Mission Activity of the Church
ARCIC	Anglican-Roman Catholic International Commission
CCC	*Catechism of the Catholic Church*
CDF	Congregation for the Doctrine of the Faith
DV	Second Vatican Council, *Dei Verbum*, Dogmatic Constitution on Divine Revelation
EV	*Enchiridion Vaticanum*
GS	Second Vatican Council, *Gaudium et Spes*, Pastoral Constitution on the Church in the Modern World
IGPII	*Insegnamenti di Giovanni Paolo II*
IPVI	*Insegnamenti di Paolo VI*
LG	Second Vatican Council, *Lumen Gentium*, Dogmatic Constitution on the Church
NT	New Testament
OT	Old Testament
PL	*Patrologia Latina*
SC	Second Vatican Council, *Sacrosanctum Concilium*, the Constitution on the Sacred Liturgy
ST	Thomas Aquinas, *Summa Theologica*

Bible References are mainly taken from the *Revised Standard Version*, except where they appear as part of a quotation from another author, in which case the author's version is retained.

PART I

CHAPTER I

The Church's Self-Understanding

A crisis of her self-understanding is, for Ratzinger, one of the greatest problems the Church faces at the present time. He pinpoints, often mercilessly, the multifaceted challenges confronting the contemporary Church, all of which are, in his view, linked to this need. One of these is the shadow of her past history, which, according to Ratzinger, in the face of a questioning generation, has left her far too defensive and thus unsure of her true identity. Of course, he is not against the acknowledgement of guilt for some incidents in the Church's history or the curtailing of a certain sense of triumphalism. He admits that 'it was both necessary and good for the Council to put an end to the false forms of the Church's glorification of self on earth and, by suppressing her compulsive tendency to defend her past history, to eliminate her false justification of self'.[1] But this ought not to be to the detriment of the truth or to kill 'our joy in the reality of an unbroken community of faith in Jesus Christ. We must rediscover that luminous trail that is the history of the saints and of the beautiful – a history in which the joy of the gospel has been irrefutably expressed throughout the centuries.'[2] Warning against a 'dangerous new triumphalism', he notes: 'So long as the Church is in pilgrimage on the earth, she has no ground to boast of her own works .... The place of the Church on earth can only be near the cross.'[3] On the other extreme, however, at the Second Vatican Council there was an obvious apologetic stance, or 'excruciating plumbing of her own depths', as Ratzinger witheringly describes

1   J. Ratzinger, *Principles of Catholic Theology: Building Stones for a Fundamental Theology* (San Francisco, CA: Ignatius Press, 1987), 373.
2   Ibid.
3   Ratzinger and Messori, *The Ratzinger Report*, 13.

it, resulting mainly from an over-concentration on the whole 'arsenal of complaints' against her.[4] In his words: 'The Council understood itself as a great examination of conscience by the Catholic Church.'[5] 'It wanted ultimately to be an act of penance, of conversion. This is apparent in the confessions of guilt, in the intensity of the self-accusations that were directed, not only to the more sensitive areas, such as the Reformation and the trial of Galileo, but were also heightened into the concept of a Church that was sinful in a general and fundamental way and that feared as triumphalism whatever might be interpreted as satisfaction with what she had become or what she still was.'[6] Excessive carefulness not to offend has led to a mentality that was overly self-condemnatory, and which sought, and saw, only the good in the other.[7] In Ratzinger's view, 'such a radical interpretation of the fundamental biblical call for conversion and love of neighbour led not only to uncertainty about the Church's own identity, which is always being questioned, but especially to a deep rift in her relationship to her own history, which seemed to be everywhere sullied. In consequence, a radically new beginning was considered a pressing obligation.'[8]

To acknowledge faults in the Church's history (which ought not to be seen in isolation from the intrinsic holiness which always belongs to her), does not preclude the truth of her being and essence. Ratzinger puts it like this: 'Penance is a necessity for both the individual and the community. But Christian penance means not self-rejection, but self-discovery.'[9] According to him, it does not entail the loss or destruction of one's identity but its discovery and affirmation in truth. Against the Gnostic teaching, which turned penance into 'a hatred of mankind, a hatred of their own lives, a hatred of reality', he insists that 'the inner precondition for penance is precisely the affirmation of oneself, of reality as such'.[10] An exaggerated

---

4   Cf. Ratzinger, *Principles of Catholic Theology*, 371.
5   Ibid.
6   Ibid.
7   Cf. ibid., 371–372.
8   Ibid., 372.
9   Ibid.
10   Ibid.

humility could be pretentious, inimical to truth and, indeed, a form of pride. Thus, Ratzinger cautions: 'Wherever the fundamental Yes to being, to life, to oneself, ceases to exist, penance disappears and turns into arrogance. For penance presumes that man is permitted to affirm himself. By its very nature, it is a penetration to the Yes in the hidden places of whatever obscures the Yes. That is why true penance leads to the gospel, that is, to joy – even to joy in oneself.'[11] Thus, the apathy, lethargy and even negativity, often witnessed within the Church today, seem linked with a lingering uncertainty relative to her identity. Hence, it is not surprising that Ratzinger hails Mary's 'yes', that authentic self-abnegation which is, in the end, the true self-affirmation, as a paradigm and a seminal fount for the Church. This is a central concern of his and, indeed, of this book.

Paradoxical as it may seem, self-doubt in the modern Church is clearly linked to what Ratzinger sees as naïve optimism about a wholly renovated world which is commonplace both within the Church and outside it. Commenting on the influences of these forces in the early post-Vatican II days, Ratzinger states: 'I am convinced that the damage that we have incurred in these twenty years is due, not to the "true" Council, but to the unleashing within the Church of latent polemical and centrifugal forces; and outside the Church it is due to the confrontation with a cultural revolution in the West: the success of the upper middle class, the new "tertiary bourgeoisie", with its liberal-radical ideology of individualistic, rationalistic and hedonistic stamp.'[12] This apparently 'brave new world', he notes, has insinuated a 'break in historical consciousness, the self-tormenting rejection of the past, that produced the concept of a zero hour in which everything would begin again and all those things that had formerly been done badly would now be done well'.[13] With the rejection of the Church's history comes the confusion of her true identity, and so a certain torpor, tedium and even rebellion, in the midst of general mayhem and uncertainty. Hence, there is a glaring need for self-awareness and definition.

---

11   Ibid., 372–373.
12   Ratzinger and Messori, *The Ratzinger Report*, 30.
13   Ratzinger, *Principles of Catholic Theology*, 372.

Peacefulness only comes through a 'positive relationship to history' and the finding of 'a better balance'.[14]

Ratzinger is principally known, especially outside the Church, for identifying the threat of a tyrannical secularism, an aggressive relativism, which repudiates, denies, or wilfully bypasses objective truth. He maintains that: 'In an age of the secular State and of Marxist messianism, in an age of worldwide economic and social problems, in an age when the world is dominated by science, the Church, too, faces anew the question of her relationship with the world and its needs. She must relinquish many of the things that have hitherto spelled security for her and that she has taken for granted. She must demolish long-standing bastions and trust solely to the shield of faith.'[15] However, Ratzinger is adamant that this in no way means that she should relinquish the root and fundamentals of her existence. It cannot imply that 'she no longer has anything to defend or that she can live by forces other than those that brought her forth: the blood and water from the pierced side of the crucified Lord (Jn 19:31–37).'[16] In the face of the relativizing of truth, the Church is called upon to confidently take her stand, and reflect ever more steadily 'on that which, in the lapse of time, has remained the one constant. To seek it without distraction and to dare to accept, with joyful heart and without diminution, the foolishness of truth', is an inalienable duty.[17] This, Ratzinger insists, is 'the task for today and for tomorrow: the true nucleus of the Church's service to the world, *her* answer to "the joy and hope, the grief and anguish of the men of our time" (*Gaudium et spes*, 903).'[18] Truth is a fundamental premise, a given, on which the essence of the Church is predicated. Imprecision relative to the nature of the Church only fosters the prevailing relativism and over-exaggerated pluralism, and vice versa. Ratzinger observes this link between objective truth and the Church's identity, as he bemoans 'the scepticism regarding

14   Ibid., 373.
15   Ibid., 391.
16   Ibid.
17   Cf. ibid., 393.
18   Ibid.

man's capacity for truth and [...] the consequent loss of the true conception of Church as well as [...] the leveling of hope to earthly history alone'.[19]

Furthermore, Ratzinger emphasizes that proper self-understanding is essential for any effective dialogue between the Church and the world or other Christians or religions, since 'dialogue is possible only on the foundation of a clear identity. One can, one must be "open", but only when one has something to say and has acquired one's own identity.'[20] He goes on to upbraid those who diminish this sense of identity: 'My impression is that the authentically Catholic meaning of the reality "Church" is tacitly disappearing, without being expressly rejected. Many no longer believe that what is at issue is a reality willed by the Lord himself. Even with some theologians, the Church appears to be a human construction, an instrument created by us and one which we ourselves can freely reorganize according to the requirements of the moment.'[21] Ratzinger's view is that no meaningful dialogue or even encounter with the world can be conducted on these assumptions.

Hence, Ratzinger's diagnosis is that there is a crisis; a crisis 'of faith and of the Church'. He concludes: 'As I shall explain in great detail, my diagnosis is that we are dealing with an authentic crisis and that it must be treated and cured.'[22] It is mainly a problem of self-identity. As Messori notes, there are no doubts in the then Cardinal Ratzinger's mind that 'the alarm must focus before all else on the crisis of the understanding of the Church, on ecclesiology'. The effects of the crisis are far-reaching for, in the words of Ratzinger, 'herein lies the cause of a good part of the misunderstandings or real errors which endanger theology and common Catholic opinion alike'.[23] The aftermath of the Second Vatican Council makes the need for a firm self-understanding even more necessary for the Church. As Ratzinger notes, 'Cardinal Julius Döpfner once remarked that the Church of the post-conciliar period is a huge construction site ... where the blueprint had been lost and everyone continues to build according to his taste.

19   Ratzinger and Messori, *The Ratzinger Report*, 23.
20   Ibid., 35.
21   Ibid., 45.
22   Ibid., 34.
23   Ibid., 45.

The result is evident.'[24] Addressing the clergy of Rome in 2013, Ratzinger highlighted the unfortunate effects of the clash between the true Vatican II Council and the virtual Council of the media, which owing to its glaring distance from the actual documents of the Council, seemed an 'imaginary Vatican III'.[25]

The remedy, however, according to Ratzinger, is the very documents of Vatican II, properly understood: 'For this healing process, Vatican II is a reality that must be fully accepted [...] as a base on which to build solidly. Hence, it is obvious that return to the documents is of special importance at the present time: they give us the right instrument with which to face the problems of our day. We are summoned to reconstruct the Church, not *despite*, but *thanks* to the true Council.'[26] The solution, for him, lies especially in that document – *Lumen Gentium* – which was one of the most controversial of the Council, as if signalling that within it lies the centre of the Church's greatest contemporary challenge.

Here it is significant that Mariology, by a vote at the Council, was placed as 'the culmination of the Dogmatic Constitution on the Church'.[27] In Ratzinger's thoughts, this ought to have been, and should still be, the resolution point of the Church's identity crisis: 'By inserting the mystery of Mary into the mystery of the Church, Vatican II made an important decision which should have given a new impetus to theological research.' On the contrary, sadly, the early post-conciliar period saw a sudden decline or nearly a collapse of Mariology and its fecund link to ecclesiology. Ratzinger, however, almost three decades later, welcomed what he called 'the signs of a new vitality'.[28] Messori avers Ratzinger's certitude of its remedial potency: 'To the crisis in the understanding of the Church, to the crisis of morality, to the crisis of woman, [Ratzinger] has a specific remedy, among others, to propose, "that has concretely shown its effectiveness

---

24   Ibid., 30.
25   Cf. Pope Benedict XVI, *Meeting with the Parish Priests and the Clergy of Rome* (14 February 2013), in: <http://www.vatican.va/content/benedict-xvi/en/speeches/2013/february/documents/hf_ben-xvi_spe_20130214_clero-roma.html>.
26   Ratzinger and Messori, *The Ratzinger Report*, 34.
27   Ibid., 104.
28   Ibid.

throughout the centuries". He presents "a remedy whose reputation seems to be clouded today with some Catholics but one that is more than ever relevant". It is the remedy that he designates with a short name: *Mary*.'[29] 'Unless one looks to the Mother of God' declares John Paul II in the same vein, it is 'impossible to understand the mystery of the Church'.[30]

This last quotation poses the question why this book is based on the Mariology of Ratzinger, and not, for instance, that of St John Paul II? I have more than once been asked this question. The answer to that, I would say, is in the question itself. John Paul II is a known Mariologist. The fact that it is thought that Ratzinger has no substantial Mariology makes this task worth undertaking.[31] My earlier research on Ratzinger opened my eyes to how his Mariology, which is indeed not considerable if judged by the number of words, has an almost infinite potency to penetrate and influence every part of theology. One might say the same thing about the few mentions of the Blessed Virgin in the New Testament, which though small are infinitely resonant and revelatory. There is a deep relationship between the Blessed Virgin Mary and the Church, a relationship which, drawn from the Scriptures, has been attested to by the Fathers of the Church, and many Christian writers throughout the Church's history. Ratzinger not only points out the same relationship, and opens up an interpretative access, a

---

29 Ibid.

30 John Paul II, Pope, *Mulieris Dignitatem*, 22.

31 With many authors, especially since his pontificate, dwelling on the life and thoughts of Ratzinger, one finds little or no mention of Mariology. We must make exceptions here for M. H. Heim who devotes fifteen pages to this. M. H. Heim, *Joseph Ratzinger: Life in the Church and Living Theology: Fundamentals of Ecclesiology* (San Francisco, CA: Ignatius Press, 2007), 399–414. Also A. Stagliano, *Madre di Dio. La mariologia personalistica di Joseph Ratzinger* (Milano: Edizioni San Paolo, 2010); J. G. Roten, 'Mary, "Personal Concretization of the Church": Elements of Benedict XVI's Marian Thinking', *Marian Studies* 57 (2006), 243–321. In Tosatti's dictionary, for instance, I searched between *Magia* and *Matrimonio* to see if I could find a mention of Mary. Cf. M. Tosatti, Il dizionario di papa Ratzinger: Guida al Pontificato (Milano: Baldini Castoldi Dalai, 2005); See also D. Tessore, *Introduzione a Ratzinger, Le posizioni etiche, politiche, religiose di Benedetto XVI* (Napoli: Fasi Editore srl, 2005); L. Boeve and G. Mannion (eds), *The Ratzinger Reader: Mapping a Theological Journey* (New York: T&T Clark International, 2010); etc.

'layer of meaning', within which the riches of this profound ontological and functional relationship can be harnessed, but, even more so, postulates that in it lies the solution to the diagnosed contemporary crisis relative to the Church and the world. This is surely worthy of sustained attention.

As a Nigerian coming from a country with a surge of multiple Pentecostal/Evangelical movements that are, at times, aggressively inimical to the Catholic Church, and which breed, in my view, both uncertainty and syncretism because they often separate experience and theology, the need for a clear understanding of the essence of the Church, and what she is not, is vital. Having been privileged to serve in the Church in parts of Africa, Europe and America, a unitary view of the Church has become a central concern. Ratzinger's profound thoughts on the Church's self-understanding and the rediscovery of Mary's significance as central to this are a crucial aid here but one that is, in my experience, insufficiently known and used. This book is my attempt to address so far as I can, the crisis that, I think, Ratzinger accurately understood.

PART II

CHAPTER 2

Resurgence of Ecclesiotypical Mariology

It will be helpful to preface our enquiry by giving it some context. Here I follow and agree with Maximilian Heim, whose study on the theology of Joseph Ratzinger has won several awards, in observing that 'no serious survey of Ratzinger's ecclesiology can ignore the historical theological background in response to which his theology takes on its own contours'.[1]

According to Heim, Ratzinger's mature theological thought had its shaping through the tensions attending the controversies that dominated the period building up to Vatican II. Ratzinger himself indicates the need to understand these tensions when he said: 'To understand Vatican II one must look back on this period and seek to discern, at least in outline, the currents and tendencies that came together in the Council.'[2] Thus it is necessary to 'inquire into the central issues of intellectual history that, on the one hand, informed this ecclesial assembly and, on the other hand, had an important influence on Ratzinger's reception of the Council'.[3]

---

1 Heim, *Joseph Ratzinger*, 509.
2 J. Ratzinger, 'The Ecclesiology of Vatican II', in *L'Osservatore Romano*, English Edition, Baltimore, MD, 23 January 2002, 5; Cf. Pope Benedict XVI, 'The Ecclesiology of Second Vatican Council', in D. L. Schindler (ed.), *Joseph Ratzinger in Communio*, 1, *The Unity of the Church* (Grand Rapids, MI: William B. Eerdmans Publishing Company, 2010), 62–77.
3 Heim, *Joseph Ratzinger*, 509.

Twentieth-Century Polemics

The central problem here is the relationship between Marian devotions and the theology inherent in the Marian dogmas with the nature and life of the Church. This problem had been foregrounded by the emphasis on returning to and renewing Catholic theology directly from biblical and patristic sources. Many theologians were involved in this. In his exemplary article, both thorough and scholarly, on 'Mary, "Personal Concretization of the Church"', Father Johann G. Roten, a student of Joseph Ratzinger,[4] gives a comprehensive summary of the history of this awakening, in what he titles 'The Ecclesiocentric Trajectory of Mariology'.[5] He presents this as an effort to address the limitations of the solely Christocentric model which was prevalent especially before mid-twentieth-century theology. Comparing the two, he says: 'Christotypical projects may lack a degree of historical sensitivity; they may fail to consider Mary's role as member of the Church and, at times, overlook her individuality. The ecclesiotypical point of view rests – among others – on solid patristic foundations and uses typological methodology. What derives from this approach is the mirror-effect: the Church reads and explicates itself in Mary and vice versa. Mary explains the Church's relationship with Christ [...] Conversely, Mary's membership in the Church is re-established.'[6]

Especially important here was the three-year study of the French Mariological Society, which devoted its annual meetings to studying 'Mary and the Church'.[7] Prominent among the many other authors (listed also by Roten), outside the French Mariological Society, who also carried on this corrective study, were Matthias Joseph Scheeben and Otto Semmelroth. Important too were Erich Przywara (much admired by Karol Wojtyla),

---

4   And the director of the International Marian Research Institute / Marian Library at the University of Dayton, Ohio, for fifteen years and later as an instructor for the same Institute.

5   Cf. Roten, 'Mary, "Personal Concretization of the Church"', 265–274.

6   Ibid., 270–271.

7   See his presentation of the chronological presentation of the three years' volumes and the various authors in Ibid., 265–267.

who called Mary 'the inner form' of the Church, Charles Journet, who saw Mary as 'the Heart of the Church', Hugo Rahner with his study of the Fathers, Yves Congar, who in Patristic fidelity presented Mary as 'type of the Church', Henri de Lubac, who saw Mary as the 'pre-figuration of the Church', and also Müller, Balthasar and many others. These prepared the way for the theology of Vatican II and, of course, formed the setting within which Ratzinger's ecclesiological Mariology and Marian ecclesiology developed. Roten emphasizes this: 'Writing in the wake of de Lubac and Balthasar, Semmelroth and Laurentin, there is no doubt that these scholars have marked Ratzinger's Marian thinking.'[8]

It is right to say that Ratzinger's mariological stance 'takes on the configuration of ecclesiocentric typology, steeped in the rediscovery of the Mary-Church relationship in the 1950s and leading up to *Lumen Gentium*, chapter 8'.[9] R. Laurentin, writing in the 1980s, describes a less positive sequence: 'The Church has passed through great changes in these last years .... in what concerns Mary, she had been at the centre and at the summit of the pontificate of Pius XII, who consecrated the world to the Immaculate Heart of Mary (31 October 1942), then defined the Assumption (1 November 1950), promulgated her Queenship in 1954 .... When John XXIII, his successor, opened the Second Vatican Council in 1962, a number of bishops were eager to react against certain Marian excesses.'[10] The resultant conflict led to the impassioned debate and vote of 1963 as to whether the Virgin Mary should have a special text of her own or be given a place in the constitution on the Church. 'One group of the Fathers wanted this integration in order to react against a narrow, particularist, and often deforming Mariology. The other group had the impression that this integration would diminish Mary and cause her to be regarded as any ordinary member of the Church.'[11] The victorious position was that favouring the integration of Mary into the treatise on the Church.

---

8 Ibid., 274.
9 Ibid., 275.
10 R. Laurentin, 'Mary and African Theology', in R. Laurentin et al. (eds), *Mary in Faith and Life in the New Age of the Church* (Ndola: Franciscan Mission Press, 1983), 29. Cf. R. Laurentin, *The Second Vatican Council and Marian Devotion*, in R. Laurentin et al. (eds), *Mary in Faith and Life*, 107–129; Heim, *Joseph Ratzinger*, 107–108.
11 Ibid.

Thereby, the two notions of Mary's proper place in theology and hence whether she should or should not have a separate document of her own, were addressed by the insertion of the Marian figure and mystery into the treatise on the Church.[12] Ratzinger saw this as one of the Council's achievements in that it 'restored to the ordered unity of the faith an isolated Mariology'.[13] Mariology, instead of being a source of division and an obstacle or a cog in the wheel of Christian unity, not only found its place in that unity of the faith, but became a path to it. Mariologists like Semmelroth, with a Patristic mindset, had already about the same time prepared this 'marriage' of Mariology and ecclesiology. He proposed that the tract on the Church 'should be placed between Christology and grace, exactly where the doctrine of Mary is generally treated today'.[14]

This 'Ecclesial Mariology' of Vatican II has, since then, been featured in the Church's teachings and liturgy as seen, for example, in the missal, and especially in papal documents.

As *Marialis Cultus* attests:

> We have the theme of Mary and the Church, which has been inserted into the texts of the Missal in a variety of aspects, a variety that matches the many and varied relations that exist between the Mother of Christ and the Church. For example, in the celebration of the Immaculate Conception which texts recognize the beginning of the Church, the spotless Bride of Christ. In the Assumption they recognize the beginning that has already been made and the image of what, for the whole Church, must still come to pass. In the mystery of Mary's motherhood they confess that she is the Mother of the Head and of the members-the holy Mother of God and therefore the provident Mother of the Church.[15]

12   For a history of the controversies, debates and voting on the document *Lumen Gentium*, Cf. G. Philips, 'Dogmatic Constitution on the Church: History of the Constitution', in H. Vorgrimler, et al. (eds), *Commentary on the Documents of Vatican II*, vol. 1 (New York: Herder and Herder, 1967), 105–137; O. Semmelroth, 'The Role of the Blessed Virgin Mary, Mother of God, in the Mystery of Christ and the Church', in *Commentary on the Documents of Vatican II* (New York: Herder and Herder, 1967), 285–286; Laurentin, *The Second Vatican Council and Marian Devotion*, 230–235.
13   Ratzinger, *Principles of Catholic Theology*, 370.
14   O. Semmelroth, *Mary Archetype of the Church* (Dublin: M. H. Gill and Son Limited, 1963), 12.
15   Pope Paul VI, *Marialis Cultus*, 11.

Lumen Gentium, itself, authorized this movement, in stating that 'the Mother of God is a type of the Church' and setting her out as the exemplar for the Church in an eminent and singular fashion.[16] This was followed almost immediately by Paul VI's teaching in *Signum Magnum* that 'Mary is the Mother of the Church – not only because she is the mother of Jesus Christ … but also because she "shines as the model of virtues for the whole community of the elect"'.[17] She is the 'fully perfected figure of the Church'[18] and her model.[19] She is 'the type of the virginity and motherhood of the total Church' and 'the sign … for the pilgrim People of God'.[20] She is placed in the heart of the Church as the figure of 'a Woman, who in a hidden manner and in a spirit of service' watches over and looks after the Church, the family of God.[21]

Vatican II is unique in that, 'there for the first time the Church took herself comprehensively as her theme in her own self-understanding'.[22]

---

16 Cf. LG 63; Pope John Paul II, *Apostolic Letter for the 1600th Anniversary of the First Council of Constantinople and the 1550th Anniversary of the Council of Ephesus*, 25 March 1981, 11, in *IGPII*, IV, 1 (1981), 815–828; LG 53, 63–68.

17 Pope Paul VI, *Signum Magnum, Apostolic Exhortation on Venerating and Imitating the Virgin Mary, Mother of the Church and Model of All Virtues*, 13 May 1967, 6, EV 2, 1177–1193; Cf. Pope Paul VI, *Marialis Cultus*, Introduction; See also number 19, Her 'miraculous motherhood, set up by God as the type and exemplar of the fruitfulness of the Virgin-Church, which "becomes herself a mother …. For by her preaching and by baptism she brings forth to a new and immortal life children who are conceived by the power of the Holy Spirit and born of God." The ancient Fathers rightly taught that the Church prolongs in the sacrament of Baptism the virginal motherhood of Mary.'

18 Ibid., 21; Cf., *RM*, 42–47.

19 Cf. ibid., 14–15, 21, 26–27, 31, 36; 'Sacred Congregation for the Clergy', *General Catechetical Directory*, 18 March 1971, 68; Pope Paul VI, *Marialis Cultus*, 4, 16, 21, 22, 36, 56; SC., 7; Pope Paul VI, *Gaudete in Domino, Apostolic Exhortation on Christian Joy*, 9 May 1975, EV 5, 1243–1313; *RM*, 2, 5, 37, 42–43, 47.

20 Ibid., 68; Cf. LG 63–65, 69.

21 Cf. Pope Paul VI, *Marialis Cultus*, Introduction.

22 Here Maximillian H. Heim quotes Olegario González Hernández, his co-winner of the Ratzinger Price in 2011. Cf. Heim, *Joseph Ratzinger*, 21. The very first paragraph of the document already accentuates this goal: 'Since the Church is in Christ like a sacrament or as a sign and instrument both of a very closely knit union with God and of the unity of the whole human race, it *desires now to unfold more fully to*

Hence the Council's document on the Church, *Lumen Gentium*, is aptly called the 'principal document of Vatican II'.[23] Gérard Philip, a peritus of the Belgian bishops at the Council and a significant member of the Preparatory Theological Commission, comments: 'There has been a general impression, since the Second Vatican Council, that the dogmatic declaration on the Church would be the great achievement of the Council. And it is still unlikely today that any of the other texts will cause the constitution *Lumen Gentium* to recede into the background. This is rather the vitally important centre to which the other decrees must be referred, and they must all be read in the light of the mystery of the Church.'[24]

However, Ratzinger laments that one of the greatest crises that has beset the Church, and the foundation of many, if not all, of her problems, lies in the right or wrong understanding and application of that momentous event and document (Vatican II and *Lumen Gentium*) in the life of the Church. The original division inside the Council as to the place of Mary in the Church has persisted, in his view, in the more than half-century following it. Ratzinger devotes much of his often-astonishing intellectual energy both to diagnosing this and showing that the Council's decision, reflected in the document, provided a genuine cure rather than creating this division. As Mary helps in safeguarding the unity of the structure of the person and nature of Jesus,[25] so also does she play an important role in the formation of Jesus – head and mystical body, the Church. In this chapter, then, we shall see how Ratzinger helps us in the proper understanding of this ecclesial Mariology, and, equally important, what image of the Church emerges therefrom.

---

the faithful of the Church and to the whole world its own inner nature and universal mission' [emphasis mine]. LG 1.

23   Cf. ibid., 25. Heim references Allois Grillmeier's submission that *Lumen Gentium* is 'a synthesis of the understanding of the Church in the past and today and the product of various movements in the present'.

24   Philips, 'Dogmatic Constitution on the Church', 105.

25   Cf. M. Schmaus, 'Mariology', in *Sacramentum Mundi: An Encyclopedia of Theology*, Vol. 3 (New York: Herder and Herder, 1969), 377.

The Trajectory of the German School of Ecclesiology

Once again, we will need some context which Ratzinger himself gives us. The first chapter of his *Introduction to Christianity* notes and deplores the dominance of historical criticism together with the rejection of metaphysics and the metaphysical which characterized much of philosophical thought in the nineteenth century. When, following the path prepared by Descartes and developed by Kant, the Italian philosopher Giambattista Vico reformulated the Scholastic equation *verum est ens* (being is truth) to *verum quia factum* ('that is to say, all that we can truly know is what we have made ourselves'), a massively radical change was set in motion.[26]

Ratzinger was tutored in this by the German Tübingen School whose theological tenets are clearly seen in the teachings of J. S. Drey, the school's first director, as described by Pioppi.[27] Certain characteristics mark this group of academics. They sought to create a theology that was in harmony or dialogue with the culture of the time. Hence, history plays a big role in their theologizing.[28] They sought a fundamental idea on which to found a theological synthesis based on Scripture and the Fathers of the Church. Their desire was to overcome any projection of Christianity as a merely

---

26 Cf. J. Ratzinger, *Introduction to Christianity* (San Francisco: Ignatius Press, 2004), 59. For more details on this, Cf. Heim, *Joseph Ratzinger*, 510–514.

27 J. S. Drey, 'contends that Christianity is not only an idea, a doctrine, but also a story: attempting therefore to overcome a theology that is anchored only on a metaphysico-deductive system; even though this history, being sacred history, has its own proper characteristics because it is guided by the divine design which, though eternal, makes itself explicit in time. […] He keeps a distance from the scholastic conception of revelation which appears reductive to him. Revelation for him is not a communication to men of a series of truths from God, but the auto-manifestation of God himself who communicates with man […] For him the reign of God is an organism that grows, develops and evolves in history, a development which takes place in the community as a development of the initial point of departure. One notices the influences of German idealism […] on the Drey's theology.' C. Pioppi, 'Scuola di Tubinga', in G. Calabrese, P. Goyret, and O. F. Piazza (eds), *Dizionario di Ecclesiologia* (Roma: Città Nuova, 2010), 1296.

28 Ibid.

abstract reality that is consequently atemporal and static. Here they introduced the very useful concept of 'vital and living organism, the notions of historical process and development,'[29] as also seen in Newman.

So Ratzinger, 'in keeping with the tradition of the Tübingen school, [...] tries to respond to the challenge of this historical paradigm bearing the stamp of German Idealism by means of "a new approach to history as the locus of God's self-revelation"; he understands history itself as an organic whole, as salvation history, which is intrinsically characterized by the ontological priority of the universal as the expression of the True.'[30] This means that theology has to take as its hermeneutic point of departure 'the question about the unity of truth in the variety of its historical transmission.'[31] Thus, there is a blending of history and ontology. This feature of the Tübingen School, manifest in Ratzinger's thoughts, was the ground for his problem with any displacement of orthodoxy by 'orthopraxis'. As Heim observes, the 'confrontation with the primacy of orthopraxis advocated by political theologies and with theological and ecclesiological relativism (e.g. in the debate with Leonardo Boff), led to a preference for the metaphysical approach.'[32]

It is important, too, that this metaphysical presumption extends to the character of the Church. Thus, 'in ecclesiology the most important characteristic theme of the Tübingen School was that of the Church as supernatural organism.'[33] One begins to see here the roots of 'Ratzinger's shift of emphasis towards the metaphysical approach of Scholasticism', significantly manifest in his ecclesiology. One of the main representatives of this Tübingen ecclesiological outlook is Johann Adam Möhler (1796–1838). As Heim notes, along with Matthias Joseph Scheeben, he 'restated in a new way the sacramental view of the Church' as found in the writings of the Latin and Greek Fathers of the Church.[34] In his *Symbolik*, Möhler

---

29   Ibid.
30   Heim, *Joseph Ratzinger*, 513.
31   Ibid.
32   Ibid., 513–514.
33   A. Nichols, *Catholic Thought since the Enlightenment: A Survey* (Pretoria: Unisa Press, 1998), 52–53.
34   Cf. Heim, *Joseph Ratzinger*, 514–515.

describes the Church as 'an *incarnatio continua*, by way of analogy with the Incarnation of the Divine Logos', a kind of prolongation of the Incarnate Word, a 'permanent incarnation of the Son of God'.[35] He saw the Church as 'an organism whose basis is the supernatural life given by Christ', an organism that grows in time, a mystery of the divine life which is present in history and develops under the guidance of the Holy Spirit.[36] Möhler must have been no small aid to Ratzinger in the appreciation of the mystery aspect of the Church, manifest in the sacramental and pneumatological. As observed by Pioppi, commenting on Möhler's ecclesiology, the Church is the creation of the Holy Spirit who is the 'principal inspirator of the faith in the faithful and the communion of the Church'. In his ecclesiological reflections, 'the Spirit himself is the principal author of the mystical unity of the Church, which is rendered visible in the magisterial, liturgical and hierarchical unity. He defines the Church as an external structure of a living power of love; the body of the spirit of the faithful which forms in a dynamic which from interiority moves towards exteriority.'[37]

All this – we can include Scheeben (1835–1888), though Scholastic by inclination – reflects the Tübingen reaction to the extreme historicism of the nineteenth century. Scheeben also adopted the same incarnational mind frame advocated by Möhler, which, as we have seen, is also Ratzinger's. Similarly, Emile Mersch and Sebastian Tromp's ecclesiological image of the Body of Christ impacted his ecclesiological vision.[38] Subsequently, as Heim observes, 'this line of thought from patristic theology is also continued by Yves Congar, Henri de Lubac, and his "pupil" Hans Urs von Balthasar. In it the reductively historical understanding of nineteenth century is once again opened out, in that history is once again understood as salvation history, at the centre of which stands the Cross.'[39] One notices also the influence

---

35   Cf. Pioppi, 'Scuola di Tubinga', in G. Calabrese, P. Goyret, and O. F. Piazza (eds), *Dizionario di Ecclesiologia*, 515.

36   Cf. Nichols, *Catholic Thought Since the Enlightenment*, 52–53; Pioppi, 'Scuola di Tubinga', in G. Calabrese, P. Goyret, and O. F. Piazza (eds), *Dizionario di Ecclesiologia*, 1297.

37   Pioppi, 'Scuola di Tubinga', in G. Calabrese, P. Goyret, and O. F. Piazza (eds), *Dizionario di Ecclesiologia*, 1297.

38   Cf. Heim, *Joseph Ratzinger*, 514–515.

39   Ibid.

of the Lutheran theologian Oscar Cullman who, as Ratzinger will always do, highlights the eschatological tension between the 'already' and 'not yet', thus manifesting the same opening out of history. Here again the idea of history as salvation history is incorporated to remedy the closed fixation on the 'historical'. One of the greatest influences on Ratzinger, though, as Heim notes, was his teacher Gottlieb Söhngen, who introduced him both to Augustine and to Bonaventure's theology of history.[40]

Pre-Vatican II Theological Dialectics

Ratzinger was not only influenced by certain theologians but also by the dialectic between different points of view amongst pre-Vatican II theologians. This was especially so regarding the nature of the Church. These divisions are familiar enough – between tradition and innovation, the biblical-ecumenical-liturgical school of thought and the charismatic Marian school, between the local and universal Church, and the hidden Church and the visible Church. These last two were especially sensitive because of the reactions of the Eastern Orthodox Churches and the Churches of the Reformation to the concentration on papal primacy, 'Roman centralism' and the Church's visible structure, following Vatican I. Underlying all these, however, was what Ratzinger has designated as a 'God crisis'.

Not long after World War I, as Ratzinger puts it: 'Romano Guardini coined an expression that quickly became a slogan for German Catholics: "An event of enormous importance is taking place: the Church is awakening within souls".'[41] This was the happy ecclesiological climate, as Ratzinger notes, which built up to the Council. Those were, so to say, the years of the Church. He reminisces:

---

40   Cf. ibid., 515–516.
41   J. Ratzinger, *The Ecclesiology of Vatican II*, 5; Cf. Pope Benedict XVI, 'The Ecclesiology of Second Vatican Council', in D. L. Schindler (ed.), *Joseph Ratzinger in Communio*, 62.

Today, it is difficult to communicate the enthusiasm and joy this realization gen-erated at the time. In the era of liberalism that preceded the First World War, the Catholic Church was looked upon as a fossilized organization, stubbornly opposed to all modern achievements. Theology had so concentrated on the question of the primacy [of Rome] as to make the Church appear to be essentially a centralized or-ganization that one defended staunchly but which somehow one related to from the outside. Once again it became clear that the Church was more than this.[42]

Ratzinger considered therefore that the consensus feeling among the German bishops, and indeed throughout the Catholic Church, was that the Church ought to be the theme of the Council. Since 'the First Vatican Council was unable to complete its ecclesiological synthesis', having been cut short by the Franco-Prussian War (1870–1871), it was exigent that the project be completed. Vatican I's isolated chapter on the primacy and in-fallibility of the Roman Pontiff had not helped the image of the Church in an overly liberalized age that already saw the Church as authoritarian and overbearing.[43] Ratzinger lucidly describes this exigency:

To offer a comprehensive vision of the Church seemed to be the urgent task of the coming Second Vatican Council. The focus on the Church flowed from the cultural atmosphere of the time. The end of the First World War had brought a profound theological upheaval. Liberal theology with its individualistic orientation was com-pletely eclipsed, and a new sensitivity to the Church had been arising. Not only did Romano Guardini speak of a reawakening of the Church in souls. The Evangelical Bishop Otto Dibelius coined the formula 'the century of the Church', and Karl Barth gave to his dogmatic synthesis of the reformed (Calvinist) tradition the program-matic title *Kirchliche Dogmatik* (Church Dogmatics). He explained that a dogmatic theology presupposes the Church, without the Church it does not exist. Among

---

42   Ratzinger, *The Ecclesiology of Vatican II*, 5; Cf. Pope Benedict XVI, 'The Ecclesiology of Second Vatican Council', in D. L. Schindler (ed.), *Joseph Ratzinger in Communio*, 63.

43   Ratzinger, however, corrects this impression, noting that 'the First Vatican Council had in no way defined the pope as an absolute monarch. On the contrary, it pre-sented him as the guarantor of obedience to the revealed Word.' Ratzinger, *The Spirit of the Liturgy*, 166.

the members of the German Episcopal Conference there was consequently a broad consensus that the theme of the Council should be the Church.[44]

There was therefore both an internal movement as a new consciousness of the Church budded within the hearts of the faithful and the external pressure to address the prevalent 'Church crisis'.

The Council Fathers at Vatican II were certainly aware of these currents and saw it as their task to attend to them. For instance, Ratzinger notes how the concerns of Orthodox and Protestant theology were 'integrated into a more ample Catholic understanding'. As a matter of fact, 'in Orthodox theology the idea of Eucharistic ecclesiology was first expressed by exiled Russian theologians in opposition to the pretensions of Roman centralism. They affirmed that insofar as it possesses Christ entirely, every Eucharistic community is already, *in se*, the Church. Consequently, external unity with other communities is not a constitutive element of the Church.'[45] For them, therefore, 'unity with Rome is not a constitutive element of the Church'. While 'such a unity would be a beautiful thing since it would represent the fullness of Christ to the external world', it is not an essential element 'since nothing would be added to the totality of Christ'.[46] Worse still, within the Protestant outlook, Luther had denied that the Spirit of Christ is in the universal Church, which for him was clearly 'an instrument of the anti-Christ', as Ratzinger observes.[47] For Luther, the Protestant State Churches of the Reformation were not really Churches but 'only social, political entities necessary for specific purposes and dependent on political powers – nothing more'. This was because 'according to Luther the Church existed in the community. Only the assembly that listens to the Word of God in a specific place is the Church. He replaced the word "Church"

---

44 J. Ratzinger, *The Ecclesiology of the Constitution on the Church, Vatican II, 'Lumen Gentium'*, in *L'Osservatore Romano*, English Edition, Baltimore, MD, 19 September 2001, 5.

45 Ratzinger, *The Ecclesiology of Vatican II*, 5; Cf. Pope Benedict XVI, 'The Ecclesiology of Second Vatican Council', in D. L. Schindler (ed.), *Joseph Ratzinger in Communio*, 67–68.

46 Ibid.

47 Ibid.

with "community" (*Gemeinde*). Church became a negative concept.'[48] The concept of Eucharistic ecclesiology, which recognizes the local gathered community within the universal communion, became a remedial clarifying model, and a key to Ratzinger's interpretation of Vatican II ecclesiology.

As we have seen, there was, alongside the 'Church crisis', a 'God crisis'. Ratzinger recalled the words of the senior Bishop of Regensburg, Bishop Michael Buchberger, to the Council Fathers: 'Dear brothers, at the Council you should first of all speak about God. This is the most important theme.'[49] Johann Baptist Metz says: 'The crisis reached by European Christianity is no longer primarily or at least exclusively an ecclesial crisis [...] The crisis is more profound: it is not only rooted in the situation of the Church: the crisis has become a crisis of God. To sum up, one could say "religion yes", "God no", where this "no", in turn, is not meant in the categorical sense of the great forms of atheism.'[50] It is rather a 'no' that is symptomatic of a loss of the sense of the mysterious, transcendent, 'Other'. In a technological world which values doing and productivity over being, the question of God increasingly rings hollow and recedes to the periphery. Ratzinger, together with all those influenced by the metaphysical (yet historical) approach of the Tübingen School, would obviously stand against this at the Council. As Heim says of him, 'God *prius* (i.e. the fact that God is prior to everything)' is 'a fundamental category of his own thinking, as opposed to praxeological approaches'.[51]

These were the problems that faced the Council, but they were faced full of hope. Yet Ratzinger rightly observes that the actual results of the Council seemed contrary to these expectations: 'Developments since the Council seem to be in striking contrast to the expectations of all, beginning with those of John XXIII and Paul VI. Christians are once again a minority, more than they have ever been since the end of antiquity.'[52] He sets this out at length in many different places. Here for instance:

48   Ibid.
49   Buchberger, cited in Ratzinger, Ibid.
50   J. Metz, cited in Ratzinger, Ibid.
51   Heim, *Joseph Ratzinger*, 520.
52   Ratzinger, *The Ratzinger Report*, 29.

What the Popes and the Council Fathers were expecting was a new Catholic unity, and instead one has encountered a dissension which – to use the words of Paul VI – seems to have passed over from self-criticism to self-destruction. There had been the expectation of a new enthusiasm, and instead too often it has ended in boredom and discouragement. There had been the expectation of a step forward, and instead one found oneself facing a progressive process of decadence that to a large measure has been unfolding under the sign of a summons to a presumed "spirit of the Council" and by so doing has actually and increasingly discredited it.[53]

Thus, Ratzinger queries: 'How was it possible for this Babylonian captivity to arise at the moment when we had been hoping for a new Pentecost? How was it possible that just when the Council seemed to have reaped the ripe harvest of the last decades, instead of enjoying the riches of fulfilment we found only emptiness? How could disintegration emerge from a great surge towards unity?'[54]

Ratzinger, unlike Roberto de Mattei and others, never blames the Council itself for its disappointing aftermath. In his opinion, 'Vatican II in its official promulgations, in its authentic documents, cannot be held responsible for this development'.[55] It is in fact contrary to and 'radically contradicts both the letter and the spirit of the Council Fathers'. Rather there is a need and obligation, against all protests, 'to show the true face of the Council'.[56] Ratzinger strongly advocates adherence to the spirit of Vatican II, provided this is based on the Council's documents. He is convinced that the post-Vatican II problems in the Church are a result of a refusal to live Vatican II as an actual historical event, attempting either to live in the past, as if the Council never happened, or to thrust forward impatiently to the future with an unfounded optimism erroneously predicated to the Council: 'Vatican II today stands in a twilight. For a long time it has been regarded by the so-called progressive wing as completely surpassed and, consequently, as a thing of the past, no longer relevant to the present.

53   Ibid., 29–30.
54   J. Ratzinger, 'Why I Am Still in the Church', in H. U. von Balthasar and J. Ratzinger (eds), *Two Say Why*, (London and Chicago: Search Press Ltd and Franciscan Herald Press, 1971), 68.
55   Ratzinger, *The Ratzinger Report*, 30.
56   Ibid., 33.

By the opposite side, the "conservative" wing, it is, conversely, viewed as the cause of the present decadence of the Catholic Church and even judged as an apostasy from Vatican I and from the Council of Trent. Consequently, demands have been made for its retraction or for a revision that would be tantamount to a retraction.'[57]

Ratzinger takes neither of these lines: 'I have always tried to remain true to Vatican II, to this *today* of the Church, without any longing for a *yesterday* irretrievably gone with the wind and without any impatient thrust toward a *tomorrow* that is not ours.'[58] This has to be, since Vatican II, though pastoral rather than dogmatic in intention, has exactly the same authority as previous Councils with which it is in real continuity. Ratzinger is very precise about this: 'Vatican II is in the strictest continuity with both previous councils and incorporates their texts word for word in decisive points.'[59] Hence, repeatedly, he insists on the need 'to *return to the authentic texts of the original Vatican II'*. Anything else would suggest a break and an abandonment of tradition, which was never the case.[60] No one has put this more forcefully than him: 'There is, instead, a continuity that allows neither a return to the past nor a flight forward, neither anachronistic longings

---

57 Ibid., 28.
58 Ibid., 19.
59 Ibid., 28. Hence Ratzinger draws two conclusions contra 'progressivism' on one side and 'traditionalism' on the other: *First*: 'It is impossible ("for a Catholic") to take a position *for* Vatican II but *against* Trent or Vatican I. Whoever accepts Vatican II as it has clearly expressed and understood itself, at the same time accepts the whole binding tradition of the Catholic Church, particularly also the two previous councils. And that also applies to the so-called "progressivism", at least in its extreme forms.' *Second*: 'It is likewise impossible to decide *in favour* of Trent and Vatican I but *against* Vatican II. Whoever denies Vatican II denies the authority that upholds the other two councils and hereby detaches them from their foundation. And this applies to the so-called "traditionalism", also in its extreme forms.' 'Every partisan choice destroys the whole (the very history of the Church) which can exist only as an indivisible unity.' Ibid., 28–29.
60 'There is no "pre-" or "post-" conciliar Church: there is but one, unique Church that walks the path toward the Lord, ever deepening and ever better understanding the treasure of faith that he himself has entrusted to her. There are no leaps in this history, there are no fractures, and there is no break in continuity. In no wise did the Council intend to introduce a temporal dichotomy in the Church.' Ibid., 35.

nor unjustified impatience. We must remain faithful to the *today* of the Church, not the *yesterday* or *tomorrow*. And this today of the Church is the documents of Vatican II, without *reservations* that amputate them and without *arbitrariness* that distorts them.'[61]

It is striking that this view of the Council is intimately bound up with Ratzinger's understanding of Mary's relation to the Church. In these concluding words of his commentary on Vatican II, made at the opening of the pastoral congress of the diocese of Aversa, he clearly identifies the being of the Church with the being of Mary:

> 'As everyone knows, the question of dedicating a specific document to Mary was widely debated. In any event I believe it was appropriate to insert the Marian element directly into the doctrine on the Church. In this way the point of departure for our consideration is once more apparent: the Church is not an apparatus, nor a social institution, nor one social institution among many others. It is a person. It is a woman. It is a Mother. It is alive. A Marian understanding of the Church is totally opposed to the concept of the Church as a bureaucracy or a simple organization. We cannot make the Church, we must be the Church. We are the Church, the Church is in us only to the extent that our faith more than action forges our being. Only by being Marian, can we become the Church. At its very beginning the Church was not made, but given birth. She existed in the soul of Mary from the moment she uttered her fiat. This is the most profound will of the Council: the Church should be awakened in our souls. Mary shows us the way.'[62]

In this remarkable statement, we see the remedial reunion of Mariology and ecclesiology made possible by the personalistic approach to both. The nature, mission of and ministry in the Church are seen in their proper perspective, as not organization-modelled but wholly Marian and 'yes'-modelled, that is, worship-shaped and aimed at holiness. The essentials of Ratzinger's mariological thinking, as I have elaborated in *Mary, Daughter Zion* and shall further expound in exploring the ecclesial implications, are all contained here.

---

61   Ibid., 31.
62   Ratzinger, *The Ecclesiology of Vatican II*, 5; cf. J. Ratzinger, *Church, Ecumenism and Politics* (Slough: St Paul's Publications, 1988), 28.

CHAPTER 3

Main Ecclesiological Models of Vatican II

There are several possible ecclesiological models of the Church.[1] We need to identify, especially, the main ones that came into play at the Second Vatican Council. These are the background to Ratzinger's corrective polemic and sustained act of thinking.

Pilgrim People of God and Mystical Body of Christ

Ratzinger argues that, in the preconciliar era, 'reflection on the Mystical Body of Christ marked the first phase of the Church's interior rediscovery'.[2] This notion was already present in St Paul. In the period immediately before Vatican II, it was re-articulated; 'the presence of Christ and the dynamics of what is alive (in Him and us)' were placed in the foreground once again. Thereby came the recognition and experience of the Church as 'something within us – not as an institution outside us but something that lives within us'.[3] Guardini masterfully couched this experience in the phrase 'the Church is awakening within souls'. Explaining this more fully, he emphasized that the Church 'is not an institution devised and built by men … but a living reality …. It lives still throughout the course of time. Like all living realities it develops, it changes … and

---

1   Avery Dulles has, in his famous theological treatise, outlined a number of these. Cf. A. Dulles, *Models of the Church* (New York: Doubleday, 1974).

2   J. Ratzinger, cited in G. Mannion, 'Understanding the Church: Fundamental Ecclesiology', in L. Boeve and G. Mannion (eds), *The Ratzinger Reader*, 102; Ratzinger, *The Ecclesiology of Vatican II*, 5.

3   Ibid.

yet in the very depths of its being it remains the same; its inmost nucleus is Christ …. To the extent that we look upon the Church as organization … like an association … we have not yet arrived at a proper understanding of it. Instead, it is a living reality.'[4]

Ratzinger, in an obvious alliance with Guardini and Tübingen School of Theology (1820–1890), notes that 'if until that time we had thought of the Church primarily as a structure or organization, now at last we began to realize that we ourselves were the Church. The Church is much more than an organization: it is the organism of the Holy Spirit, something that is alive, that takes hold of our inmost being.'[5] It is this realization, Ratzinger says, that soon found expression in the biblical concept of the 'Mystical Body of Christ'. Though a rich and valuable concept, with time the concept of the Church as the 'Body of Christ' received both further refining and interpretation but also some contestation. This came in two directions. One was from Henri de Lubac's incorporation of the riches of Orthodox Eucharistic ecclesiology, which filtered in through Russian theologians exiled from 1917. The other was the criticism of the idea of the 'Mystical Body of Christ' in the 1930s, by some German theologians who proposed, instead, the Old Testament and Augustinian concept of 'People of God'.[6]

It was these pressures that led to the Council endorsing both the concept of the Mystical Body of Christ and the Old Testament sense of Israel as the 'People of God' as equally applicable to the Church. Where, as Ratzinger presents it, the image of the Mystical Body appeared 'too narrow a starting point to define the many forms of belonging to the Church now found in the tangle of human history', the 'People of God' proved instrumental for attending to this in *Lumen Gentium* 15 and 16. 'If we use the image of a body to describe "belonging" we are limited only to the form of

---

4   R. Guardini, cited in Ratzinger, *The Ecclesiology of Vatican II*, 5; Cf. Pope Benedict XVI, 'The Ecclesiology of Second Vatican Council', in D. L. Schindler (ed.), *Joseph Ratzinger in Communio*, 63; cf. R. Guardini, *La Chiesa del Signore* (Brescia: Morcelliana, 1967), 160.

5   Ratzinger, *The Ecclesiology of Vatican II*, 5; Cf. Pope Benedict XVI, 'The Ecclesiology of Second Vatican Council', in D. L. Schindler (ed.), *Joseph Ratzinger in Communio*, 62–77.

6   Ibid.

representation as "member". Either one is or one is not a member, there are no other possibilities. One can then ask if the image of the body was too restrictive, since there manifestly existed in reality intermediate degrees of belonging.[7] On the contrary, the concept of 'the People of God' was seen as more effective in describing 'the relationship of non-Catholic Christians to the Church as being "in communion" and that of non-Christians as being "ordered" to the Church'.

This had some less fruitful consequences. Ratzinger set them out brusquely enough: 'In the early stages of the reception of the Council, the concept of "People of God" predominated together with the theme of collegiality; the term "people" was understood in terms of ordinary political usage, later in the context of liberation theology it was understood in terms of the Marxist use of the term people as opposed to the dominating classes, and even more widely, in the sense of the sovereignty of the people, which would now finally be applied to the Church.'[8] These 'verbal fireworks', as Ratzinger calls them, quoting Norbert Lohfink, tended towards a certain sense of Western 'democratization' or Eastern European 'popular democracy'. Hence, the idea of People of God was interpreted purely horizontally as opposed to its full, original, meaning which is indeed rich and effective for ecclesiology. This is certainly Ratzinger's view, and he outlines the advantages that made it useful at the Council. Firstly, it served as 'an ecumenical bridge'. Especially between Catholics and Protestants. Protestants disliked the prevalent idea of 'the Body of Christ' advanced within the Catholic Church, which depicted the Church as 'Christ who continues to live on earth', as 'the incarnation of the Son that continues to the end of time'.[9] For the Protestants, this amounted to the Church identifying herself with Christ. It was necessary to stress that 'the Church is not identical with Christ, but she stands before Him. She is a Church of sinners, ever in need of purification and renewal'.[10] Furthermore, according to Ratzinger, the concept of the Pilgrim People of God, properly understood, has an 'eschatological' import, unveiling as it does the truth that, as

7   Ibid.
8   Ratzinger, *The Ecclesiology of the Constitution on the Church*, 5.
9   Ibid.
10   Cf. Ratzinger, 'The Ecclesiology of Vatican II', 5.

a pilgrim people, the Church's 'true and proper hope still lies ahead of her'. It secures, too, the unity of salvation history, linking Old and New, Israel and the Church, in her pilgrim journey. It equally expresses the Church's unity amid the variety of peoples, ministries and services.[11] Despite its merits, this rather uncommon biblical image can lend itself to exaggeration or abuse. Ratzinger cites approvingly the balanced account given by Werner Berg: 'Despite the small number of passages that contain the expression "People of God", from this point of view "People of God" is a rare biblical expression, but nevertheless a common idea emerges: the phrase "People of God" expresses "kinship" with God, a relationship with God, the link between God and what is designated as "People of God", hence a "vertical orientation". The expression lends itself less to describe the hierarchical structure of this community, especially if the "People of God" is described as a "counterpart" to the ministers … Nor, starting with its biblical significance, does the expression lend itself to a cry of protest against the ministers: "We are the People of God".'[12]

Ratzinger consummately rejects any purely horizontal, sociological, misinterpretation of the 'People of God' and warns that 'the Church does not exist for herself but must be God's instrument' pressing forward to the attainment of that goal in which 'God will be all in all' (1 Cor 15:28). Hence, he concludes: 'It was the concept of God that lost out in the "fireworks" sparked by the expression, and in this way the expression, People of God, lost its meaning. In fact, a Church that exists for herself alone is superfluous. And people notice it immediately. The crisis of the Church, as it is reflected in the concept of People of God, is a "crisis of God"; it is the consequence of abandoning the essential. What remains is merely a struggle for power.'[13] As in feminism, where it is often forgotten that the virtues of Mary are proposed to us all, first and foremost, in a vertical dimension; that is, in terms of man and woman in relation to God, and not necessarily woman in relation to man, here again a wholly horizontal interpretation forces the Church into a contradiction of whom she is called to be.

11   Cf. Ibid.; cf. Pope Benedict XVI, 'The Ecclesiology of Second Vatican Council', in
       D. L. Schindler (ed.), *Joseph Ratzinger in Communio*, 62–77.
12   W. Berg cited in Ibid.
13   Ibid.

In Pauline ecclesiology, the basic difference between the New Testament Church and the Old Testament 'pilgrim people of God' is captured in the term 'Body of Christ'. This Pauline designation expresses the fact that 'Church is, not an organization, but an organism of Christ'.[14] This notion helps to assure the right understanding of the nature of the Church as not just a people, society, or structure. Even Mary is rightly called the 'people of God'.[15] Hence, Church is indeed the 'people of God', so long as it is properly understood. If the Church becomes a people at all, says Ratzinger, it must be in the context of the body of Christ, in the sense of the Eucharistic assembly constituted through his death and resurrection. Becoming a member of the Church, he notes, is not by, or a matter of, sociological adherence but, rather, is by an incorporation into the Body of Christ 'through baptism and the Eucharist'. The problem is that 'behind the concept of the Church as the People of God, which has been so exclusively thrust into the foreground today, hide influences of ecclesiologies which de facto revert to the Old Testament; and perhaps also political, partisan and collectivist influences [...] The Church does not exhaust herself in the "collective" of the believers: being the "Body of Christ" she is much more than the simple sum of her members.'[16] Such wrong ecclesiologies inherently constitute a danger, that of 'abandoning the New Testament in order to return to the Old'. It ought not to be forgotten that ' "People of God" in Scripture, in fact, is a reference to Israel in its relationship of prayer and fidelity to the Lord. But to limit the definition of the Church to that expression means not to give expression to the New Testament understanding of the Church in its fullness [...] the Church receives her New Testament character more distinctively in the concept of the "Body of Christ" '.[17]

Any worldview in which little or no recognition is given to the metaphysical will, Ratzinger thinks, overlook the mystery aspect of the Church.

---

14   J. Ratzinger, 'Thoughts on the Place of Marian Doctrine and Piety in Faith and Theology as a Whole', in H. U. Von Balthasar – J. Ratzinger, *Mary: The Church at the Source* (San Francisco: Ignatius Press, 2005), 26.

15   Ratzinger, *Daughter Zion*, 43.

16   Ratzinger and Messori, *The Ratzinger Report*, 47.

17   Ibid.

Hence, today, man 'could experience the greatness of the Sacred as a burden and long (even unconsciously) to free himself from it, lowering the mystery to his human stature, instead of abandoning himself to it with humility but with trust, so as to lift himself up to that height'.[18] The mystery dimension of the Church, by which it 'is a reality that surpasses, mysteriously and infinitely, the sum of her members',[19] secures, and is, as well, guaranteed by, the understanding of the Church as the mystical Body of Christ. Ratzinger here re-affirms the thrust of Pius XII's encyclical *Mystici Corporis* (1943) which he sees as in no way displaced by the Council's sanctioning of the 'People of God'.

As earlier noted, one of the criticisms against the formulation 'Body of Christ' as opposed to the 'People of God', is that it so identifies the Church with Christ that she becomes immune to criticism. It did not take too long for even Catholic theologians to observe that the concept, strictly taken, portrays the Church as all divine, denying her human element, to the point that it makes 'her every declaration and ministerial act so definitive that it made any criticism appear to be an attack on Christ himself'.[20] Hence, there was a need to accentuate the Christological distinction between Christ and the Church. This can be found in Thomas Aquinas' theory of participation (in the light of which God and creatures can share in being analogously without a breach of God's transcendence and unicity).[21] This theory, which proved useful in preserving the metaphysical distinction between the Creator and creatures, is no less effective here. The dialogical relationship between God and his creatures, as often stressed by Ratzinger, as I demonstrated in the hermeneutic of the 'yes' of Mary,[22] proves vital here too. If the dialogical import of the 'yes' of Mary plays a significant role in the spousal identity of the Church, it does so all the more in the understanding of her designation as the 'Body of Christ'. It saves the concept of

18   Ibid., 58.
19   Ibid., 52.
20   Cf. Ibid.; cf. Pope Benedict XVI, 'The Ecclesiology of Second Vatican Council', in D. L. Schindler (ed.), *Joseph Ratzinger in Communio*, 62–77.
21   St Thomas Aquinas, *Summa Contra Gentiles*, II, ch. 15, a. 4; St Thomas Aquinas, *Summa Theologica*, I, q.44, a. 1–3.
22   I have explored this earlier in *Mary, Daughter Zion*.

the 'Body of Christ' from a tendency towards a 'Christomonism'; in the sense of 'an absorption of the Church, and thus of the believing creature, into the uniqueness of Christology'.[23] Ratzinger highlights how this is safe-guarded in the reciprocity of the same spousal link. For, 'in Pauline terms … the claim that we are the "Body of Christ" makes sense only against the backdrop of the formula of Genesis 2:24: "the two shall become one flesh" (1 Cor 6:17)'.[24] The dialogical relation in the 'yes' of Mary offers the inter-pretative key for proper understanding and expression of the identity of the Church as the 'Body of Christ' in the 'dynamism of a unity that does not abolish dialogical reciprocity'.[25] 'By the same token', says Ratzinger, '… the Eucharistic-Christological mystery of the Church indicated in the term "Body of Christ" remains within the proper measure only when it includes the mystery of Mary: the mystery of the listening handmaid who – liberated in grace – speaks her *Fiat* and, in so doing, becomes bride and thus body'.[26] Mary is indeed without fault and the Church, founded and sustained by her 'yes', is always the spotless Bride of Christ. The Creed includes belief in '*sanctam Ecclesiam*'. But the Church is also the pilgrim 'People of God' orientated to God in worship but, like Israel itself, errant and peccant in its members. Like Mary, the Church is 'full of grace' but its members, even the apostles and saints, will never be immaculate like her.

Eucharistic Ecclesiology

Roten suggests that, in Ratzinger's view, Eucharistic ecclesiology is 'a faithful synthesis of Vatican II's most important intentions regarding the doctrine on the Church'.[27] What are the relations between the Eucharist

---

23 J. Ratzinger, 'Thoughts on the Place of Marian Doctrine', in H. U. von Balthasar and J. Ratzinger (eds), *Mary: The Church*, 26.
24 Ibid.
25 Ibid.
26 Cf. ibid., 26–27.
27 Roten, 'Mary, "Personal Concretization of the Church"', 259.

and Church? De Lubac, who had some reservation about the normal understanding of the Church as the Body of Christ, argued that the term '*corpus mysticum*' originally referred to the Eucharist.[28] Ratzinger agrees: 'For St Paul and the Fathers of the Church the idea of the Church as the Body of Christ was inseparably connected with the concept of the Eucharist.'[29] There is clearly a significant link between the *Corpus Christi mysticum* and the *Corpus Christi sacramentum*. St Augustine, for instance, saw that the Christian's 'Amen' to the Eucharist is an assent to what he truly is – a member of the Body of Christ.[30] There is an intrinsic link between the two. Hence, Ratzinger himself aptly describes the Mass as the Church's constitution.

It is not difficult to connect this insight to the logic of our discussion so far. The zenith and centre of the 'yes', both of Christ and of Mary, was on the Cross. So also, the peak and the core of the Church's 'yes' ought to be in the Mass which is the celebration of her ultimate 'yes' with, and to, Christ. The Mass necessarily becomes the fullest expression of her true identity since it is the Eucharistic image of the 'Body of Christ', sign and reality, which manifests that the Church lives as, and is nothing other than, true worship offered to God and in union with him. The Psalmist's declaration, placed on the lips of Christ by the author of the letter to the Hebrews – 'Sacrifices and offerings thou hast not desired, but a body hast thou prepared for me; in burnt offerings and sin offerings thou hast taken no pleasure. Then I said, Lo, I have come to do thy will, O God, as it is written of me in the roll of the book' (Heb 10:5–10) – applies to Christ's body, the Church.

---

28   J. Ratzinger, *The Ecclesiology of Vatican II*, 5; Cf. Ratzinger, *Church, Ecumenism and Politics*, 17; Cf. Pope Benedict XVI, 'The Ecclesiology of Second Vatican Council', in D. L. Schindler (ed.), *Joseph Ratzinger in Communio*, 62–77.

29   Ibid.

30   'If you are the body and members of Christ, then it is your sacrament that you receive. To that which you are you respond "Amen" ("yes, it is true!") and by responding to it you assent to it. For you hear the words, "the Body of Christ" and respond "Amen". Be then a member of the Body of Christ that your Amen may be true.' St Augustine, Sermo 272: PL 38, 1247; CCC. 1396.

The image of the Eucharistic Body of Christ manifests the Church's real being and life as authentic worship. It shows, too, both her realized unity and her mission towards unity. In the *kenosis* and immolation of the Body of Christ on the Cross, which the Church relives in the celebration of her Eucharist, the promised unity of all heaven and earth is disclosed.[31] This is already eschatologically realized but, in the present history of the Church Militant, it is the pledge of the unity of the entire creation. If we use Ratzinger's favourite biblical, agricultural description (the grain's self-surrender to death), there is no longer isolation and loss but a harvest of many. The 'many', as St Paul teaches in 1 Corinthians 10:17, are one body (just as the grains and grapes that inseparably form the Eucharistic bread and wine).[32] Thus, Eucharistic ecclesiology gives concreteness to the image of the Church as the 'Body of Christ'. It uncovers its sacramental character, which reveals and conceals, depicts a concreteness and yet reserves a mystery. As the forms of bread and wine retain their texture, colour, corruptibility and other properties, so the Church, as the mystical 'Body of Christ', remains truly human and historical.

This gives us, too, a vantage point from which to understand the relationship between the particular and universal Church. Just as Mary's 'yes' was not an isolated and private experience, so is the faith of the Christian in Christ. We do not and cannot stand alone in our belief, neither as individuals nor as isolated groups. The Christian 'faith is not an individual, solitary act, a response of the individual. Faith means to believe *together*, with all the Church'.[33] Even though the fullness of Christ is realized, as the

---

31   This understanding grounds Ratzinger's belief that God's *kenosis*, his exemplary self-emptying/immolation, is the point of unity, the place where all religions can unite without claims of supremacy. Cf. J. Ratzinger, *Many Religions – One Covenant*, 108.

32   On this Ratzinger rightly states: 'the Eucharist is instrumental in the process by which Christ builds himself a Body and makes us into one single Bread, one single Body. The Eucharist is thus understood entirely in a dynamic ecclesiological perspective. It is the living process through which, time and time again, the Church's activity of becoming the Church takes place. The Church is Eucharistic fellowship. She is not just a people: out of many peoples of which she consists there is arising one people, through the one table that the Lord has spread for us all.' J. Ratzinger, 'We Who Are Many Are One Body (1 Corinthians 10:17)', in S. O. Horn – V. Pfnür (eds), God is *Near Us: The Eucharist, the Heart of Life* (San Francisco: Ignatius Press, 2003), 114–115.

33   Ratzinger, *The Ratzinger Report*, 33.

Church's teaching, helped by influences from Orthodox Eucharistic ecclesiology, emphasizes, in the Eucharistic assembly, yet this truth must have,
as an integral element, the unity and singleness of the person of Christ in
all times and places.

Ratzinger always insists on the logical and ontological priority of
the universal Church over particular Churches. He robustly defends the
decree of the Congregation for the Doctrine of the Faith on this matter,[34]
against its critics:

> This ontological precedence of the universal Church, the one Church, the one body,
> the one bride, over the concrete empirical realizations in the particular Churches
> seems to me so obvious that I find it hard to understand the objections to it. Indeed
> it seems to me that they are only possible if one does not want to see, or no longer
> succeeds in seeing, the great Church conceived by God – perhaps out of desperation
> at her earthly inadequacy –; she now appears as a theological fancy, so all that re
> mains is the empirical image of the Church in the mutual relations and conflicts of
> the particular Churches [...] If from now on the Church can only be recognized in
> her human organization, then, in fact, all that is left is desolation.[35]

Once again, a clear understanding of the mysterious, metaphysical
dynamics at play in Salvation history is vital. Without it, aggressive demystification and myopic historicism efface the place of the universal and
every idea of real unity. This is where the importance of the primacy of the
logos cannot be underestimated. The *Logos*, the person of Christ, cannot be
historicized to the point of limitedness. He is not just Jesus of Nazareth,
shut up within the confines of his direct and immediate place, words and
actions in time. He is truly God the Son, the Incarnate Word of God, at
once human and divine, historical and yet beyond history. The particular
and the universal, known to Greek philosophy as the One and the Many,
are not in any conflict in him. Rather, in and through him, is realized

---

34   This is 'supported concisely by recalling that, according to the Fathers, the Church,
     which is one and unique precedes creation and gives birth to the particular
     Churches' A. Roberts and J. Donaldson, 'Some Aspects of the Church Understood
     as Communion', *Letter to the Bishops of the Catholic Church*, 28 June 1992, 9.
35   Ratzinger, *The Ecclesiology of the Constitution on the Church*, 5. The resonance of the
     Tübingen idea of the ontological priority of the universal as an expression of the
     true cannot be mistaken.

the healing of the rupture in that primordial link. Christ is both one and many, Alpha and Omega, within sequence and beyond all sequence, truly *Logos Incarnatus*.

This makes the Incarnation in the womb of Mary a focal point in universal history, a particular point of the convergence of all being – earthly, human and divine. When the Church understands herself as a 'maturing' of the Incarnation experience, a prolongation of the 'yes' that is the centre of the world and of every authentic unity, it becomes easier for her to grapple with other attendant questions relative to her here and now existence. That the Mass is the Church's form, according to Ratzinger, 'means that through it she develops an entirely original relationship that exists nowhere else, a relationship of multiplicity and of unity'.[36] Hence, it is primarily in the Eucharistic celebration that integration and harmony within the Body of Christ, which is at once particular and universal, one and offered 'for many', is wholly achieved as the very life of the Church and as eternal life: 'In each celebration of the Eucharist, the Lord is really present. He is risen and dies no more. He can no longer be divided into different parts. He always gives Himself completely and entirely.'[37] Ratzinger tellingly quotes here the statement of the Council Fathers that 'this Church of Christ is truly present in all legitimate local communities of the faithful which, united with their pastors, are themselves called Churches in the New Testament. For in their locality these are the new People called by God, in the Holy Spirit and with great trust (cf. 1 Thess 1:5) …. In these communities, though frequently small and poor, or living in the diaspora, Christ is present, and in virtue of His power there is brought together one, holy, catholic and apostolic Church' (*Lumen Gentium*, n. 26).[38]

Is there some contradiction in Ratzinger's thought here? How does one reconcile 'the primacy of the particular over the universal',[39] as we saw in Chapter One, with this priority of the universal Church over particular Churches? Only a comprehensive appreciation of Ratzinger's doctrine of

36 Ratzinger, *The Ecclesiology of Vatican II*, 5.
37 Ibid.
38 Cf. Ibid.; LG 26.
39 Cf. Chapter 1.

the primacy of the *logos*, as set out in the first chapter, will resolve this conflict. For it is a false dichotomy.

Christian teaching on the *Logos*, unlike its Hellenistic antecedent, is marked by that insistence upon the personal element, characteristic of all Ratzinger's Mariology and ecclesiology. In Christianity, the *Logos* is a person. The universal has wholly entered into the particular in a non-competitive, conciliatory fashion. The concept of the person, even though particular, implies openness to the universal. Indeed, the universal and the particular meet in the person. Marian ecclesiology, embedded in the personal, represents, indeed liberates us, from this conflict between the particular and the universal Church. With the truth of the Church as a person, there can be no totally isolated particular Church, completely independent of the universal Church. But the reverse is also true. The idea of a universal Church that is not particularized is exactly only that, an idea, an abstraction. Neither can be truly Church. For, the Church is a person, and so unites the two.

Ratzinger applies this same unifying clue to the conflict between collegiality and personality which he sees as particularly relevant to our time: 'Collegiality is one principle of what is genuinely Christian and ecclesial: personality is the other. It is one of the lessons of this decade that only a proper balance of the two can create freedom and fecundity.'[40] A good instance of this necessary harmonization is found in the Benedictine Rule, which Benedict deeply admires (he took his name from both Benedict XV and St Benedict). It keeps this careful balance between the powers of the abbot and the community in chapter, the exigencies of the Rule and the proper insights of individual persons. Such balance is only achieved to the extent that collegiality does not kill personality but is an expression of personality truly realized. Freedom, that essential part of personhood, is always requisite. The life of the Holy Trinity, where there is perfect unity and yet three persons, is the ultimate paradigm here. It is not an abstruse doctrine but the transcendent participatory foundation of the Church's universal and particular life. In this way, we can understand how there is no contradiction between the priority of particularity in Mary's 'yes' to

---

40   Ratzinger, *Principles of Catholic Theology*, 375.

the birth of the *Logos* in her and the priority of the universal Church over particular church which has its origins in her 'yes'.

Ecclesiology of Communion

Linked with the sacramental dimension of the image of the mystical 'Body of Christ' is the concept of the ecclesiology of communion. The link, according to Ratzinger, 'is absolutely explicit in St Paul: "The cup of blessing which we bless, is it not a communion in the blood of Christ? The bread which we break, is it not a communion in the body of Christ? Because there is one bread, we who are many are one body ..." (1 Cor 10:16ff). The ecclesiology of communion at its very foundation is a Eucharistic ecclesiology.'[41] The twentieth anniversary of Vatican II saw an attempt being made to more fully connect the various strands of its ecclesiology. This attempt brought together the image of the 'Body of Christ', the sacramental dimension, the Eucharist and the concept of 'People of God'. What stands out is mankind's union with Jesus Christ through the Church. Ratzinger proclaims that this 'fellowship (*communio*) among men is born here and merges into fellowship (*communio*) with the One and Triune God'. And the 'the goal of all this is the fullness of joy', revealing the eschatological dynamic in the bosom of the Church.[42] Unity leads to joy – the goal of the Christian journey. Little wonder that the greeting of the Annunciation, to her who had become the tabernacle of that unity, the seminal Church, was an invitation to joy – 'Rejoice'.

However, much like the concept of the 'People of God', Ratzinger was very aware that the ecclesiology of communion was not immune from similar misinterpretation, devaluation and distortion: 'As happened to the concept "People of God", one must point to a growing horizontal understanding that abandoned the concept of God. The ecclesiology of communion was reduced to a consideration of relations between the local Church

41 Ratzinger, *The Ecclesiology of Vatican II*, 5.
42 Ibid.

and the universal Church [...] Naturally the egalitarian thesis once more gained ground: only full equality was possible in "communio". Here again was the exact same argument that had exercised the disciples about who was the greatest amongst them.'[43]

Ratzinger identifies this as the same 'God crisis' that is always the bane of the Church; that constant tendency to turn away from the face of the Lord, to disconnect from God, to run away from his mystery. It is still the same hiding from the Lord, which was the aftermath of craving equality with God in the Garden of Eden, and which occasioned the redemptive promise of the New Eve and the New Adam. Once this crisis is present, the victim is always that unity which is founded on, and guaranteed by, that all determinant vertical relation, the God-man relation. A deep understanding of Mary as our model in faith is, again, Ratzinger's remedy to this disruption. The woman, to whom the 'Allness' of God was not a threat, whose total submission makes her a living grace, is *salus infirmorum*, 'vanquisher of all heresies'. Just as all these problems are connected – the denial of metaphysics, the God crisis, excessive masculine activism and autarchy – so do the solutions converge in one woman who epitomises all that the Church is meant to be. Hence, in Ratzinger's understanding, the last part of *Lumen Gentium*, culminating in that final chapter, which is dedicated to the Mother of God, is the summary of whom the Church is called to be, her true identity. It is thus an apropos ending to this chapter and a good introduction to the next, best given by Ratzinger himself:

> In these chapters the inner goal of the Church, the most essential part of its being, comes once again to the fore: holiness, conformity to God. There must exist in the world space for God, where he can dwell freely so that the world becomes His 'Kingdom'. Holiness is something greater than a moral quality. It is the presence of God with men, of men with God; it is God's 'tent' pitched amongst men in our midst (cf. Jn 1:14). It is a new birth – not from flesh and blood but from God (Jn 1:13). Orientation towards holiness is one and the same as eschatological orientation [...] The Church exists to become God's dwelling place in the world, to become 'holiness'. This is the only reason there should be any struggle in the Church – and not for precedence or for the first place.[44]

---

43   Ibid.
44   Ibid.

PART III

CHAPTER 4

Ratzinger on the Marian Nature of the Church

It is extremely important, too, that Ratzinger's main mariological writings, as he himself attests, are mostly a response to the after-effects of Vatican II's incorporation of the Marian treatise into ecclesiology.[1] Why is this so? There are two main reasons.

Firstly, the victory of the biblical-ecumenical-liturgical school over the Marian school at the Council[2] seemed a defeat of Mariology. It 'brought about a decision whose significance can hardly be overestimated'.[3] Secondly there ensued a misunderstanding that seemed to place Mariology at loggerheads with biblical and Patristic fidelity and so enthrone an exaggerated Biblicism that could be said to have toed the line of Josef Rupert Geiselmann's question concerning the material 'sufficiency' of Scripture.[4] This authorized a historicism that looked primarily backwards, as if the more ancient, therefore the more true and reliable, 'as if the Church were not alive and therefore capable of development in every age'.[5] Ratzinger saw in this a revival of the opening that, at the beginning of the Twentieth Century, gave birth to Modernism. With the Church placed in the past, and the past apparently far from reach, free experimentation of every kind to fill the vacuum created in the present, defines the modern climate. Again, the understanding of Mary in relation to the Church, sound in itself, was given an extreme interpretation that almost dissolved Mariology into an abstract, impersonal and socio-structural ecclesiology.[6] 'In fact', says Ratzinger, 'the

---

1   Ratzinger, *Daughter Zion*, 7.
2   As earlier discussed, under the title *Twentieth-Century Polemics*, in Chapter 2.
3   J. Ratzinger, 'Thoughts on the Place of Marian Doctrine', in H. U. von Balthasar and J. Ratzinger (eds), *Mary: The Church*, 22.
4   Ibid., 23.
5   Ibid., 24.
6   Cf. Ibid., 27.

immediate outcome of the victory of ecclesiocentric Mariology was the collapse of Mariology altogether.[7] The Church was progressively seen, no longer in the Patristic personal vision but as a structure, a programme of action (as in the 'Jesus Program' and the post-conciliar occasional concentration of religious feeling on political change, especially in Latin America), or at best, once again as *Societas perfecta*. The dissolution of Mariology, of her who is 'the Church in person' into the society-Church or structured organization meant a deathblow to both a true Mariology and true ecclesiology.

Ratzinger is always courteous and modest, but he fights this tooth and nail. He argues that the intentions of the Council cannot be understood in this way. What is needed is careful attention to the documents of the Council. He notes especially the fact that Chapter 8 of *Lumen Gentium*, which is on Mary, was written in such a way as to correspond intrinsically to the chapters dealing on the structure of the Church (Chapters 1–4). The point of this correspondence was either wrongly understood or totally overlooked, so much so that the 'actual historical effect contradicts its original meaning'. Paul VI was fully aware of this, too, hence his 'corrective' apostolic letter, *Marialis Cultus*, of 2 February 1974.[8] Ratzinger's Mariology could be seen as the meditated continuation of Paul VI's document, based on the Patristic Marian heritage that helped shape the earliest ecclesiology. This will emphasize the personal nature of the Church as opposed to a social or structural model. For the latter, besides contradicting the Patristic wisdom, trashes the development confirmed by the Council itself of the displacement of the notion of *Societas perfecta* by an emphasis on the mysterious and sacramental nature of the Church. It will amount to an unfortunate hither and thither movement. Luther and the Protestant Reformation's rejection of the visible church and her mediation and authority had met with the equally strong response of the Counter Reformation theologians (led by Robert Bellarmine), couched in image of the church as *Societas Perfecta* which emphasized the visible church and its hierarchical structure. As I have already shown, the nineteenth and twentieth centuries saw an effort to complement this image with the biblical and

7   Ibid., 24.
8   Cf. Ibid., 24–25.

Patristic understanding of the mystery element of the church in which the Tübingen School played leading role. Almost contemporaneously, there was the awakening of the consciousness of the, also, Patristic ecclesiotypical Mariology, thus highlighting the interrelatedness of Mary and the Church. The Marian dimension proves a remedy to ecclesiological identity crisis, just as Mariology finds its balance in Mary's corelation with the Church. This is the true hermeneutic of the 'yes' of Mary, which I have explored in *Mary, Daughter Zion*, for which the Mariology contained therein is a remedy to radical misunderstandings of the Church at all times, and especially now. Ratzinger puts it bluntly: 'Here I see the truth of the saying that Mary is the "vanquisher of all heresies".'[9]

It is time to set out the main lines of what could be seen as Ratzinger's polemic, which is nothing other than a giant corrective to misunderstandings, attributed to the Council but not generated or authorized by it. I will do so by gathering together some of the principal terms of his theology that I have examined in the first volume, *Mary, Daughter Zion*.

Reciprocal Mirrors: Mary, the Church as a Person and in Person

As we have seen, the concept of person plays a big role in the Mariology and anthropology of Ratzinger. It is also a key concept in his ecclesiology. In the Godhead, person allows for the community of the Father, the Son and the Holy Spirit. In man, it opens the way for relations between man and God and among men. It assures at one and the same time both individuality and community. It secures the link between the particular and the universal. His ecclesiology, just as his Mariology,[10] could be termed personalistic. In his Mariology, Mary's 'yes' is her identity and she is the Church in person. Therefore Mary's 'yes' is the expression of what or who the Church is. The words of Ignace de la Potterie that 'in her real person

9   Ibid., 27.
10   Cf. Staglianò, *Madre di Dio* (already cited).

there is an anticipation which will be realised for the new people of God, the Church',[11] are relevant here. In the Incarnation, she became God's tent and 'the beginning of the holy Church.'[12] Thus there is a real link between the virgin of Nazareth and the Church of the New Covenant, the universal Church, and the link is not just extrinsic, but inherent and ontological.

Hence, Ratzinger argues that 'everything said about *ecclesia* in the Bible is true of her, and vice versa: the Church learns concretely what she is and is meant to be by looking at Mary. Mary is her mirror, the pure measure of her being.'[13] The Church is, as it were, coextensive with Mary. The movement ought to be from entity to person and not from the person of Mary to a structure. In Ratzinger's ecclesiology, this is always the recommended, indeed indispensable, process. It is in accord with his position on the primacy of the *logos* and its implications. He says: 'Mariology can never simply be dissolved into an impersonal ecclesiology. It is a thorough misunderstanding of patristic typology to reduce Mary to a mere, hence, interchangeable, exemplification of theological structures. Rather, the type remains true to its meaning only when the non-interchangeable personal figure of Mary becomes transparent to the personal form of the Church herself.'[14] For 'in theology, it is not the person that is reducible to the thing, but the thing to the person. A purely structural ecclesiology is bound to degrade church to the level of a program of action.'[15]

Here, we see then, the clearest possible condemnation of the effects of the aftermaths of Vatican II on Mariology and emergent notion of the Church. He gives a concrete example of how this process ought to function with the doctrine of the Immaculate Conception. Here the Scriptural

11   I. De La Potterie, *Mary in the Mystery of the Covenant* (New York: Alba House, 1992), 262.

12   J. Ratzinger, 'Et Incarnatus est de Spiritu Sancto ex Maria Virgine', in H. U. von Balthasar and J. Ratzinger, *Mary: The Church*, 93–94.

13   J. Ratzinger, 'Hail Full of Grace: Elements of Marian Piety According to the Bible', in H. U. von Balthasar and J. Ratzinger, *Mary: The Church*, 66.

14   Ibid., 27.

15   J. Ratzinger, 'Thoughts on the Place of Marian Doctrine' in H. U. von Balthasar and J. Ratzinger, *Mary: The Church*, 27.

(Ep 5:27) and Patristic teaching concerning the *Ecclesia immaculata*, which was the earliest anticipation of the doctrine of the Immaculate Conception, found concrete existence in the person of Mary. It was transferred to Mary and not vice versa.[16] For Ratzinger, if those assertions that were actually a typologically developed ecclesiology were transferred to the concrete figure of Mary, 'this means that Mary is presented as the beginning and the personal concreteness of the Church'.[17] Just as the Word, the pre-existent *Logos* finds personal concreteness in Jesus Christ, and not vice versa. The attempt to reduce Mary to a certain ideological, abstract and sociological structure called Church, is like attempting to reverse the Incarnation by turning Christ into mere Word (some sort of 'De-incarnation'). The wisdom of the Fathers 'proclaims that this new Israel (which is simultaneously the true old Israel, the holy remnant preserved by the grace of God) is not only an idea, but a person. God does not act with abstractions or concepts; the *type*, of which the ecclesiology of the New Testament and the Fathers speak, exists as a *person*.'[18] And this 'transfer' is not arbitrary. That is to say that it is not by an unfounded designation that Mary, and no other, emerges as the personification of *immaculata* who constitutes the antithesis new-old Israel. It is significant that Ratzinger finds the justification for it in the Adam-Christ type and in 'the Lucan equation of the true daughter Zion with the listening-believing Virgin' in the Annunciation Narrative, as taught by the Fathers, especially Irenaeus.[19] Hence, even the Evangelist was aware of this fulfilment of the Old Testament type in Mary. A true hermeneutics of Mary's 'yes' makes this clear. The Immaculate Conception finds its true explanation in that correspondence of the total 'yes' of Mary with the 'yes' of God.

The implication then is that what applies to Mary ought to apply to the Church. Mariology becomes normative for a proper ecclesiology, as

16   Ratzinger, *Daughter Zion*, 67.
17   Ibid., 67–68.
18   Ibid., 68; 'God does not deal with abstractions. He is a person, and the Church is a person.' J. Ratzinger, 'Hail Full of Grace', in H. U. von Balthasar and J. Ratzinger, *Mary: The Church*, 66.
19   See my exposition of this theme in *Mary, Daughter Zion*.

it is for all of theology. The Church looks to Mary and to her 'yes' for her true identity; or rather she is truly herself in this identification with Mary.[20]

Ratzinger's argument is addressed to the post-Vatican II Church, but it is not novel. Blessed Isaac of Stella said: 'In the inspired Scriptures, what is said in a universal sense of the virgin mother, the Church, is understood in an individual sense of the Virgin Mary, and what is said in a particular of the virgin mother Mary is rightly understood in a general sense of the virgin mother, the Church. When either is spoken of, the meaning can be understood of both, almost without qualification.'[21] *Lumen Gentium*, too, acknowledges that 'in the most holy Virgin the Church has already reached that perfection whereby she is without spot or wrinkle'.[22] This has obvious implications for ecclesiology.

Shared Images

The first implication is that images of Mary are also images of the Church. We have already seen Ratzinger's use of many of them – the Church is the 'Well of the Living Water', 'The House of Prayer', 'Daughter Zion', 'Ark of the Covenant', 'The New Temple', 'The People of the New Covenant', ' The New Israel', 'The Holy Remnant', 'The New Creation', 'Grace', 'The Immaculate Conception', 'The New Eve' and 'The Holy Soil'.

One good example is the way that Ratzinger understands the figure of Mary as God's 'Holy Soil' as summarizing what he considers the proper attitude of, and to, the Church ought to be. He highlights the element of receiving as seen in the receptivity of Mary's 'yes'. Her keeping of God's word in her heart (Lk 2:19,51) further discloses her as the image of the Church, she who 'keeps God's word in her heart and passes it on to others'.[23] 'The element of "receiving"

---

20   Cf. Ibid.
21   Isaac of Stella, 'Mary and the Church', Sermon 51, Office of Readings, Second Saturday of Advent, *The Divine Office: Liturgy of the Hours According to the Roman Rite*, I (Dublin: The Talbot Press Ltd, 1974), 95; PL 194, 1863.
22   LG 65.
23   Ratzinger, *Jesus of Nazareth*, 125–126.

belongs essentially to the Church, just as faith comes from "hearing" and is not the result of one's decision or reflection […] One cannot make the Church but only receive her; one receives her from where she already is, where she is really present: the sacramental community of Christ's Body moving through history.'[24] All this, for Ratzinger, is pertinent to any notion of Church reform:

> We must always bear in mind that the Church is not ours but his. Hence, the 'reform', the 'renewals' – necessary as they may be – cannot exhaust themselves in a zealous activity on our part to erect new, sophisticated structures. The most that can come from a work of this kind is a Church that is 'ours', to our measure, which might indeed be interesting but which, by itself, is nevertheless not the true Church, that which sustains us with the faith and gives us life with the sacrament. I mean to say that what we can do is infinitely inferior to him who does. Hence, true 'reform' does not mean to take great pains to erect new facades (contrary to what certain ecclesiologists think). Real 'reform' is to strive to let what is ours disappear as much as possible so what belongs to Christ may become more visible. It is a truth well known to the saints. Saints, in fact, reformed the Church in depth, not by working up plans for new structures, but by reforming themselves.[25]

Therefore, he concludes that 'what the Church needs in order to respond to the needs of man in every age is holiness, not management'.[26] When holiness is in place, management or administration and all services also become a response, a 'yes' to God in conformity with the Logos. Orthopraxis (right practice/quotidian tasks) will flow from orthodoxy which is not just right doctrine, but right worship.

The Feminine Church (*Ecclesia*)

An important element in Ratzinger's reflections on *The Background and Significance of the Second Vatican Council's Declarations on Mariology*, is

---

24 J. Ratzinger, cited in Mannion, 'Understanding the Church', in L. Boeve and G. Mannion (eds), *The Ratzinger Reader*, 104.
25 Ratzinger and Messori, *The Ratzinger Report*, 53.
26 Ibid.

his contention that, contrary to what he has described as a masculine, activistic and merely sociological *'populus Dei'* ecclesiological notion, 'Church – *ecclesia* – is feminine'. This, according to him, means that 'Church is more than "people", more than structure and action'. This is because she is an organism, a person, a mother and bride. As Ratzinger notes, she 'contains the living mystery of maternity and of bridal love that makes maternity possible.'[27] Whether or not Ratzinger's characteristic use of grammatical gender to prove a point is sound, there is no doubt that he is consistently opposed to the tendency to downplay the feminine dimension in every area; in the reading of Scriptures, in the understanding of the Church and even in modern anthropological and general world view where, as we saw in *Mary, Daughter Zion*, even the fight for the feminine turns into an attempt to masculinize the woman, thereby paradoxically re-inscribing the apparently effaced masculine dominion. He comments acerbically: 'This attitude characterises our whole approach to the Church. We treat the Church almost like some technological device that we plan and make with enormous cleverness and expenditure of energy. Then we are surprised when we experience the truth of what St Louis-Marie Grignon de Montfort once remarked, paraphrasing the words of the prophet Haggai, when he said, 'You do much, but nothing comes of it' (Hg 1:6)![28]

The femininity of the Church primarily comes to light in the disposition of her consent; the disposition of availability of the soil for fruitfulness (maternity) and of the submission in/to bridal love (espousal). This is unprecedented in itself and yet not without precedents, for it is the summation of the feminine line running through salvation history, from Eve to the New Eve. Hence, the Marian dimension of ecclesiology 'maintains the presence of the feminine dimension of the event of salvation, whose permanent center it is. By contrast where the Church is understood only institutionally, only in the form of majority decisions and actions, there

27   J. Ratzinger, 'Thoughts on the Place of Marian Doctrine', in H. U. von Balthasar and J. Ratzinger, *Mary: The Church*, 25.
28   J. Ratzinger, 'My Word Shall Not Return to Me Empty', in H. U. von Balthasar and J. Ratzinger, *Mary: The Church*, 16.

is no room for the feminine dimension.'[29] The disposition of the Church ought to be that responsorial disposition of the New Eve to the New Adam, which is the antithesis of the first Eve-Adam type. This disposition manifests the triumph of grace which punctuates salvation history in the persons of the barren mothers.

But is it possible for the Church, the Bride of Christ, to participate in Mary's motherhood? Ratzinger seems to think that it is: 'At the moment when she pronounces her Yes, Mary is Israel in person; she is the Church in person and as a person. She is the personal concretization of the Church because her *Fiat* makes her the bodily Mother of the Lord […] We can say that the affirmation of Mary's motherhood and the affirmation of her representation of the Church are related as factum and mysterium facti, as the fact and the sense that gives the fact its meaning.'[30]

Can the Church by any means be the Mother of God? And how is the New Eve mother of the New Adam? Of course, Mary's divine maternity is not about begetting the Godhead, and even with regard to God the Son, it is not about the eternal begetting by God the Father but nativity in time. The question is rather about how to reconcile the spousal link implied in the Eve-Adam typology with maternity; how Mary, and so the Church, can be both spouse and mother in relation to Christ. This, as Ratzinger observes, is clarified only in the Lucan harmonization of the two beatitudes: 'blessed is she who believed' (Lk 1:45) and 'blessed … are those who hear the word of God and keep it' (Lk 11:28). Only here does a new kind of motherhood, or rather, the fullness of motherhood, surface – the motherhood of the 'yes', a motherhood of the *Logos*, based on the Patristic notion of Mary as the New Eve – the true 'mother of the living'. We have already considered this idea at some length in *Mary, Daughter Zion*, the antecedent to this book. It consists of becoming a holy soil whose total availability aids or occasions the germination and fruitfulness of the Word. It is the type of motherhood that Augustine talks of, and Ratzinger refers to, in his reflection on the 'yes' of Mary, saying that Mary conceived Christ

29   J. Ratzinger, 'The Sign of the Woman: An Introductory Essay on the Encyclical Redemptoris Mater', in H. U. von Balthasar and J. Ratzinger, *Mary: The Church*, 55.

30   Ratzinger, 'Thoughts on the Place of Marian Doctrine', in ibid., 30.

first in her soul before conceiving him in her body. Augustine holds that 'Mary is more blessed for perceiving the faith of Christ than for conceiving the flesh of Christ'.[31] In this sense, the later conception does not imply any closer relation to Christ and depends upon the former. St Ambrose gives a clue to how the Church, like Mary, can be the mother of Christ when he says: 'Whatever soul has believed conceives and engenders the Word of God [...] If according to the flesh there is one mother of Christ, according to faith, nonetheless, Christ is the fruit of all. For every soul receives the Word of God, provided it is immaculate and free from vices, keeping chastity with unblemished purity.'[32] Thus, motherhood of the 'yes' of Mary is available to all. Meister Eckhart puts it more poignantly: 'We are all meant to be mothers of God, for God is always needing to be born.'[33] It is our universal call; it is the call of the Church. Blessed Isaac of Stella is particularly eloquent here:

> The whole Christ and the unique Christ – the body and the head – are one: one because born of the same God in heaven, and of the same mother on earth. They are many sons, yet one son. Head and members are one son, yet many sons; in the same way, Mary and the Church are one mother, yet more than one mother; one virgin, yet more than one virgin. Both are mothers, both are virgins. Each conceives of the same Spirit, without concupiscence. Each gives birth to a child of God the Father, without sin. Without any sin, Mary gave birth to Christ the head for the sake of his body. By the forgiveness of every sin, the Church gave birth to the body, for the sake of its head. Each is Christ's mother, but neither gives birth to the whole Christ without the cooperation of the other.[34]

Ratzinger is clearly in line with this tradition though he puts it less poetically: 'Mary's motherhood becomes theologically significant as the ultimate personal concretization of the Church.'[35] That the feminine nature of the Church has a spousal dimension is an understanding as old as the

---

31   St Augustine cited in O'Carroll, *Theotokos*, 142.
32   Ibid., 142.
33   M. Fox, *Meditations with Meister Eckhart* (Santa Fe, New Mexico: Bear and Company, Inc., 1983), 74.
34   Isaac of Stella, *Mary and the Church*, 95.
35   J. Ratzinger, 'Thoughts on the Place of Marian Doctrine', in H. U. von Balthasar and J. Ratzinger, *Mary: The Church*, 30.

Church itself.[36] But how this applies to Mary has been less articulated. Nevertheless, it is clear that the character of Mary's response resembles that of a trusting bride. Of course, Ratzinger rightly notes that Mary 'is first related to Christ, not as bride, but as mother'.[37] Yet, with Balthasar, Ratzinger sees in the 'yes' of Mary a bridal consent to love.

Ratzinger joins the Fathers in interpreting the passion of Christ as marriage: 'Not without reason did the Church Fathers interpret the passion and cross as marriage, as that suffering in which God takes upon himself the pain of the faithless wife in order to draw her to himself irrevocably in eternal love.'[38] The 'personal, albeit anonymous ecclesiology'[39] of the Fathers, which Ratzinger embraces and gives its name – Mary – implies this spousal link between Christ and Mary. It would seem that if the spousal nature of the Church does not also apply to Mary, a weakness would be established in Ratzinger's argument, which, like that of Isaac of Stella, insists on the convertibility of the two.

Some authors, apart from Ratzinger have dwelt on this theme of Mary as the bride of Christ, or 'bridal motherhood' as Scheeben prefers to express it.[40] Even though Ratzinger does not dwell systematically and extensively on this, it fits naturally into the logic of his argument. For him, the salvation accomplished by the triune God finds its hermeneutical centre or crystallization in Christ and the Church. And Church in this relationship refers to 'the creature's fusion with its Lord in spousal love',[41] which leads to divinization.

---

36 St Paul gives the basic and unequivocal teaching on the spousal relationship between Christ and the Church (Eph 5:23–32).

37 Ibid., 29.

38 Ratzinger, *Daughter Zion*, 28–29.

39 J. Ratzinger, 'Thoughts on the Place of Marian Doctrine', in H. U. von Balthasar and J. Ratzinger, *Mary: The Church*, 29.

40 Cf. Scheeben, *Mariology*, I, 154–183; Papali, *Mother of God*, 8; Nichols, *Holy Order*, 151; H. U. von Balthasar, 'Who Is the Church', in H. U. von Balthasar, *Explorations in Theology II: Spouse of the Word* (San Francisco, CA: Ignatius Press, 1991), 143–191; Semmelroth, *Mary Archetype of the Church*, 117–139.

41 J. Ratzinger, 'Thoughts on the Place of Marian Doctrine', in H. U. von Balthasar and J. Ratzinger, *Mary: The Church*, 30.

This argument makes Mary's position clear. For, it was in her and in the effect of her *fiat* – the Incarnation – that this fusion was supremely established. Thus, the quintessence of the bridal nature of individual souls, and of the entire Church, relative to Christ exists in her. This was seen exactly in this way by Blessed Isaac, 'In a way, every Christian is also believed to be a bride of God's Word, a mother of Christ, his daughter and sister, at once virginal and fruitful. These words are used in a universal sense of the Church, in a special sense of Mary, in a particular sense of the individual Christian. They are used by God's Wisdom in person, the Word of the Father.'[42]

The 'masculinization' of the Church, according to Ratzinger, reflects problems outside the Church. So, to be fair, the problem is not exclusively ecclesiological. It also has social and other mundane concomitants, outside the compass of our deliberation here. Ratzinger equally berates these, when he queries: 'What is the woman to do when the roles inscribed in her own biology have been denied and perhaps even ridiculed? If her wonderful capacity to give love, help, solace, warmth, solidarity has been replaced by the economistic and trade-union mentality of the "profession", by this typical masculine concern? What can the woman do when all that is most particularly hers is swept away and declared irrelevant and deviant?'[43] It has also wreaked havoc within the Church, most obviously in religious orders. 'Without perhaps being fully conscious of the reasons, the woman religious feels the deep disquiet of living in a Church where Christianity is reduced to an ideology of doing, according to that strictly masculine ecclesiology which nevertheless is presented – and perhaps believed – as being closer also to women and their "modern" needs.' The truth however, Ratzinger underscores, is that this is due to the jettisoning of the silence of mystery which leaves no room for mystical experience. This is indeed the 'pinnacle of religious life' offered to all but in which for centuries, and not without reason, women have blossomed more than men.[44]

---

42   Isaac of Stella, *Mary and the Church*, 95.
43   Ratzinger and Messori, *The Ratzinger Report*, 103.
44   Cf. Ibid.

In Ratzinger's view, not even the male religious is spared from this. 'Activism, the will to be "productive", "relevant", come what may, is the constant temptation of the man, even of the male religious.'[45] Hence, 'it is no accident if the word "Church" (*ecclesia*) is of feminine gender. In her, in fact, lives the mystery of motherhood, of gratitude, of contemplation, of beauty, of values in short that appear useless in the eyes of the profane world.'[46] Ratzinger sees such 'masculinization' as the fruit of wrong ecclesiologies 'that present the Church as a "People of God" committed to action, busily engaged in translating the Gospel into an action program with social, political and cultural objectives.'[47] This is also extended to the liturgy, where as we shall see, the norm seemed to have become 'the more active (that is, the busier), the better'. Ratzinger's critique of these varied wrong turns is rooted in his Mariology. And that, too, is the remedy for them.

The Church: A Marian Mystery

One component rediscovered by the 'Body of Christ' Eucharistic ecclesiology is the understanding of the Church as mystery. The God crisis, Church crisis and the crisis of woman or the loss of the feminine in an overly masculine world setting, all these are made possible and plausible, in Ratzinger's view, by the loss in theology of a sense of mystery just as philosophy is distorted by its denial of metaphysics. Heidegger, for whose thinking Ratzinger has real but qualified admiration, is an exception to this.

If this analysis is correct, the problem cannot be solved by ratiocination; rather, in Ratzinger's words: 'This is why the Church needs the Marian mystery; this is why the Church herself is a Marian mystery',[48] for

---

45   Ibid.
46   Ibid.
47   Ibid.
48   J. Ratzinger, 'My Word Shall Not Return to Me Empty', in H. U. von Balthasar and J. Ratzinger, *Mary: The Church*, 17.

it is a mystery founded on the living and life-giving 'yes' to that which ever exceeds our understanding. This is what Ratzinger refers to when he calls for a recreation of the proper climate by rediscovering 'the meaning of the Church as Church of the Lord, as the locus of the real presence of God in the world'. He echoes those 'awesomely challenging words' of Vatican II, wisely describing the Church as 'the Kingdom of Christ now present in mystery'.[49] Such a realization will disclose that behind some of the external forms of the Church, which are inevitably human constructs, there are fundamental structures and elements that are 'willed by God himself' and therefore are sacrosanct. 'Behind the *human* exterior stands the mystery of a *more than human* reality, in which reformers, sociologists, organizers have no authority whatsoever.'[50] This is one of Ratzinger's avowed reasons for fidelity to the Church, because he is convinced that, despite everything, 'at the deepest level it is not our, but His Church'.[51]

Without this understanding of the Church as mystery, it – or we should say 'she'- will be viewed, as Ratzinger notes, as merely 'a human construction, the product of our own efforts', to be modified at will. 'Even the contents of the faith', he cautions, 'end up assuming an arbitrary character', as they will lack any authentic, guaranteed conveyor.[52] The truths of the faith will be fundamentally relativized based on conveniences, times, peoples and places, since the mysterious root, that ontological guarantor of real unity, will be missing. This has implications for ministry in the Church, as we shall see.

Ratzinger does not oppose 'mystery' to 'truth' for the objectivity of truth itself requires the reality and 'authority of mystery',[53] of that ontological, impalpable principle of universality, of Ratzinger's 'layer of meaning'.[54] Indeed, as he warns, 'without a view of the mystery of the

49   Cf. Ratzinger, *The Ratzinger Report*, 48; LG 3.
50   Ratzinger, *The Ratzinger Report*, 46.
51   J. Ratzinger, 'Why I Am Still in the Church', in H. U. von Balthasar and J. Ratzinger (eds), *Two Say Why*, 80.
52   Cf. Ratzinger, *The Ratzinger Report*, 46.
53   Scott Hahn uses this expression as his theme for the presentation of the biblical theology of Benedict XVI (Ratzinger). Cf. Hahn, *The Authority of Mystery*, 97–140.
54   The layer of meaning he wishes to uncover to inspire more reflections and research. Cf. Ratzinger, *Daughter Zion*, 7–8.

Church that is also *supernatural* and not only *sociological*, Christology itself loses its reference to the divine in favour of a purely human project: the Gospel becomes the *Jesus-project*, the social-liberation project or other merely historical, immanent projects that can still seem religious in appearance, but which are atheistic in substance.'[55] Hence *Lumen Gentium's* characterization of the Church as 'present in mystery' is the *sine qua non* of authentic ecclesiology. It forestalls the above danger by securing the vital, mysterious, spiritual element intimated by the notion of the mystical body of Christ while also safeguarding the real object of the concept of *societas perfecta* by affirming her visible elements and structures as God's kingdom present on earth.

The communion of the saints is a sign of this. The Church does not exhaust herself in what is immediately visible. She includes members of all times and places, embraces all the saints (the triumphant Church) and also preserves the merits of Christ, her invisible head. Ratzinger reminds us that *Communio sanctorum* means also, and perhaps originally, 'to have "holy things" in common, that is to say, the grace of the sacraments that pours forth from the dead and resurrected Christ'. Thus, he concludes that 'it is precisely this mysterious yet real bond, this union in Life, that is also the reason why the Church is not *our* Church, which we could dispose of as we please. She is, rather, *his* Church. All that which is only our Church is not Church in the deep sense; it belongs to her human – hence secondary, transitory – aspect.'[56] The mystery of God's life in the submissive Holy Soil, Mary, epitomizes and exemplifies the Church's submission to a mysterious being and calling. Through Mary alone can she find a proper self-understanding.

55   Ratzinger, *The Ratzinger Report*, 46.
56   Ibid., 48.

The Mystery of the Church's Nativity

The Eucharistic-Sacramental, mysterious nature of the Church is clearly
intimated by her birth within the setting of the Last Supper, which
is a sacrament of the paschal sacrifice of the Cross. In Ratzinger's own
words: 'Jesus' Last Supper could be defined as the event that founded the
Church. Jesus gave His followers this Liturgy of Death and Resurrection
and at the same time He gave them the Feast of Life. In the Last Supper
he repeats the covenant of Sinai – or rather what at Sinai was a simple
sign or prototype, that becomes now a complete reality: the communion
in blood and life between God and man.'[57] Nevertheless, the birth of the
Church is not simply located at a single moment of Salvation history –
Last Supper, the Cross or Pentecost – as is often done. Rather, it is seen in
the whole of Salvation history, beginning from the loving divine thought,
through the preparatory stages in the Old Testament, to the events of
the Incarnation from the Annunciation, which saw the beginning of the
salvation-enabling 'yes', through the entire life of Jesus, to the Cross – the
peak of the communion of 'yeses'. Hence, Ratzinger's allusion to the Last
Supper as the beginning of the Church, does not present that in isolation.
For, as he observes, 'clearly the Last Supper anticipates the Cross and the
Resurrection and presupposes them, otherwise it would be an empty gesture. This is why the Fathers of the Church could use a beautiful image
and say that the Church was born from the pierced side of the Lord, from
which flowed blood and water.' Thus he concludes, 'When I state that the
Last Supper is the beginning of the Church, I am actually saying the same
thing, from another point of view.'[58]

57   Ratzinger, *The Ecclesiology of Vatican II*, 5; Cf. Pope Benedict XVI, 'The Ecclesiology
     of Second Vatican Council', in D. L. Schindler (ed.), *Joseph Ratzinger in Communio*,
     62–77; Cf. Ratzinger, *Church, Ecumenism and Politics*, 13–28. On Ratzinger's
     presentation of the exegetical debates relating to the foundational history of the
     Church, Cf. J. Ratzinger, *Called to Communion: Understanding the Church Today*
     (San Francisco, CA: Ignatius Press, 1996), 13–20.
58   Ratzinger, *The Ecclesiology of Vatican II*, 5; Cf. Pope Benedict XVI, 'The Ecclesiology
     of Second Vatican Council', in D. L. Schindler (ed.), *Joseph Ratzinger in Communio*,
     62–77; Cf. Ratzinger, *Church, Ecumenism and Politics*, 13–28.

Just as patristic teaching on Mary as the personification of a theological figure conceived in the mind of God and running through the feminine line of the Old Testament as part of the Pauline mystery to be revealed in Christ in the fullness of time, is the primal clue to Mariology, so does the Church's root in the same mind of God before creation reveal the truth about her identity. This, again, brings together and makes comprehensible as one piece, the entire history of salvation. Ecclesiology, like Mariology, is an essential part of the seamless, albeit checkered, tapestry of the unfolding of God's love in history.

The Fathers of the Church see the *ecclesia immaculata* as a person in an amazingly dramatic relationship of love with God;[59] similarly, in the celebration of the Immaculate Conception, the texts of the Roman missal, as Paul VI notes, 'recognize the beginning of the Church, the spotless Bride of Christ'.[60] The Church is herself immaculately conceived. The Church therefore keeps the Solemnity of December 8 as 'a joint celebration of the Immaculate Conception of Mary, of the basic preparation (cf. Is 11:1,10) for the coming of the Savior and of the happy beginning of the Church without spot or wrinkle'.[61]

Yet, as the paschal mystery, and its sacramental expression in the Eucharist, long prefigured in the Old Testament, are the culmination of the unison of 'yeses' (God's 'yes' to man and man's 'yes' to God in Christ through Mary), of the Immaculate Conception and Annunciation, so are they the climax of the church's origination, long foreshadowed.

59　Cf. Ratzinger, *Daughter Zion*, 67.
60　Pope Paul VI, *Marialis Cultus*, 11; Cf. *Roman Missal*, 8 December, Preface.
61　Pope Paul VI, *Marialis Cultus*, 3.

CHAPTER 5

The Liturgy: Ecclesial Self-Expression as Marian Mystery

Since the Eucharistic-Sacramental nature of the Church is implied even in her origin, one already begins to sense how, for Ratzinger, the liturgy is 'the existential expression of the Church'.[1] To place Mary in relation to the liturgy especially the Eucharist, we must first give some account of Ratzinger's ideas about the relation of liturgy and the Church. Ratzinger contends that it is in and through her worship that the church 'becomes Church'.[2] Corroborating the thrust of Vatican II's *Sacrosanctum Concilium*, he insists that the real nature of the true Church is made manifest in the liturgy.[3] Hence, according to him, 'the Church's Mass is her constitution'. This, he argues, is because the Church is essentially 'a Mass (sent out: "missa"), a service of God, and therefore a service of man and a service for the transformation of the world'.[4] Thus, the Church's identity and mission are both located in the liturgy/worship, which is the burden of the figure of the woman, Mary.[5] For, with her complete capitulation to God effecting a perfect union, Mary occasions and participates pre-eminently in the New Temple, the '*Logos* sacrifice' perfected in Christ. She, thus, exemplifies the truth

---

1   Heim, *Joseph Ratzinger*, 518.
2   Cf. ibid., 523.
3   'For the liturgy, "through which the work of our redemption is accomplished", most of all in the divine sacrifice of the Eucharist, is the outstanding means whereby the faithful may express in their lives, and manifest to others, the mystery of Christ and the real nature of the true Church.' SC 2.
4   Ratzinger, *The Ecclesiology of Vatican II*, 5.
5   I have argued this in a proceeding volume – *Mary, Daughter Zion*.

of our anthropological constitution, as Irenaeus' famous dictum – the glory of God is man fully alive – is realized in her.

Accordingly, the liturgy plays a major role in Ratzinger's thinking and obviously so in his Mariology and ecclesiology. Ultimately, 'liturgy "covers everything"',[6] since, for him, 'prayer embraces the whole world, and the world is comprehended within prayer'.[7] He agrees with Paul VI that sacred worship is 'the primary task of the People of God'.[8] Scott Hahn notes that, for Ratzinger, 'liturgy is the goal of creation and of the human person'.[9] An obvious example is his liturgical interpretation of the Annunciation context and content as indicating the inauguration of the universal *logos* sacrifice, and thus the New Temple. The second scene of the Annunciation as recorded in the Protoevangelium of James was in Mary's house, in her very unofficial room. Observing the contrast to the annunciation of John the Baptist's birth, Ratzinger underscores the latter's occurrence 'in the temple to an officially functioning priest – according to the prescribed, official disposition of the Law, linked to its cult, its local setting, and its representatives'.[10] He interprets this as signalling the transition from the old temple to the new and from the old priesthood to the true high priest.[11] It is, according to him, notably symbolic: 'The annunciation of Mary happens to a woman, in an insignificant town in half-pagan Galilee, known neither to Josephus nor the Talmud. The entire scene was unusual to Jewish sensibilities […] Thus begins a new way, at whose centre stands no longer the temple, but the simplicity of Jesus Christ. He is now the true temple, the tent of meeting.'[12] Furthermore, in the cultic language[13] of the angel's words, 'the power of the Most High will cover you with its shadow' (Lk. 1: 35), Ratzinger, characteristically, sees an evocation of the Temple of Israel

6   Ratzinger, *The Spirit of the Liturgy*, 160.
7   J. Ratzinger, 'The Church Subsists as Liturgy and in the Liturgy', in S. O. Horn – V. Pfnür (eds), God *Is Near Us: The Eucharist, the Heart of Life* (San Francisco: Ignatius Press, 2003), 122.
8   Pope Paul VI, *MarialisCultus*, 1.
9   Hahn, 'The Authority of Mystery', 136. See also GS 22.
10   Ratzinger, *Daughter Zion*, 42.
11   Cf. Ratzinger, *Jesus of Nazareth*, 18, 22, 23.
12   Ratzinger, *Daughter Zion*, 42.
13   Ratzinger, *Jesus of Nazareth*, 29.

and 'the holy tent in the wilderness, where God's presence was indicated in the cloud' (Ex 40:34; 1 K 8:11).[14]

Remarkably, this inauguration of the New Temple at the Annunciation is the culmination of a long track of Old Testament oracles and presagers to the eradication of the Old cult and establishment of authentic worship. It is thus not only linked to the long expectation of the Patriarchs, but to creation.

The New Temple (Liturgy) as the Goal of Creation and Exodus

Ratzinger looks back to the Old Testament experiences and intimations of the centrality of worship as forerunners of the Church's immersion into Mary's total attentiveness to God's Word. The trajectory goes back to creation itself. Significant here is the setting apart of the seventh day for rest and worship, which shows the entire creation as ordered towards worship: 'Creation moves toward the Sabbath, to the day on which man and the whole created order participates in God's rest, in his freedom.'[15] Thus, the very sequence of creation is symbolic. Ratzinger accentuates the occurrence of Man's creation in-between all other creatures and the Sabbath day (the Lord's Day of rest). This signalled man's role as intermediary, as it were, the 'priest' of creation. His vocation is to bring all creation to God in worshipful communion. Creation, then, is 'a space for worship', Ratzinger argues:

> To understand the account of creation properly, one has to read the Sabbath ordinances of the Torah. Then everything becomes clear. The Sabbath is the sign of the covenant between God and man; it sums up the inward essence of the covenant. If this is so, then we can now define the intention of the account of creation as follows: creation exists to be a place for the covenant that God wants to make with man. The goal of creation is the covenant, the love story of God and man .... If, then, everything is

14   Cf. Ratzinger, *Introduction to Christianity*, 272–273.
15   Ibid., 25.

directed towards the covenant, it is important to see that the covenant is a relationship: God's gift of himself to man, but also man's response to God. Man's response
to the God who is good to him is love, and loving God means worshipping him.[16]

Thus, he concludes that 'if creation is meant to be space for the covenant,
the place where God and man meet one another, then it must be thought
of as a space for worship'.[17]

It is not inapt to see here, too, how the 'ex nihilo' – God creating out
of nothing – strengthens the understanding of the liturgy as *actio divina*.
The sole agency of God in the covenantal liturgy of creation, as in the
'grace-full' enactment of the new cult/temple in Mary (Lk. 1:28, 49), is unmistakable. I have already given much attention in the preceding volume
to grace as the hermeneutic of the 'yes' and entire being of Mary, making
her *actio divina par excellence* as her Magnificat confesses – 'The Almighty
has done great things' (Lk. 1:49).

Furthermore, I think that anyone reading Ratzinger's *The Spirit of the
Liturgy* will be struck by the striking interpretation of the words of Moses
to Pharaoh: 'Let my people go, that they may serve me in the wilderness' (Ex
7:16), and by what he makes of this construal in establishing the centrality
of worship in the entire earthly project of, not only man, but all creatures;
for Moses would not even accept Pharaoh's concession to leave their properties and livestock behind while going to worship. Typically, Ratzinger
explains that the goal of the exodus is not so much the Promised Land as it
is worship: 'In all this, the issue is not the promised Land: the only goal of
the Exodus is shown to be worship, which can only take place according to
God's measure ....'[18] Thus, the exodus was a didactic liturgical procession: 'In
its wanderings, Israel discovers the kind of sacrifice God wants [...] Israel
learns how to worship God in the way he himself desires.' They learnt the
truth that true worship consists not only of cult but also of 'life according
to the will of God'[19] In other words, liturgy is correlational to being, it is
an essential constituent of the nature of God's people. Hence Ratzinger

16   Ibid., 26.
17   Ibid.
18   Ratzinger, *The Spirit of the Liturgy*, 16.
19   Ibid., 50.

alludes to the prophetic disquiet and questioning that accompanied the sacrificial system of the Old Testament in this regard, stretching even to the New Testament, recommending covenant fidelity as integral part of worship.[20] Few references will suffice here: 'behold, to obey is better than sacrifice' (1 Sam. 15:22); 'for I desire steadfast love and not sacrifice' (Hos. 6:6); 'in the day that I brought them out of the land of Egypt, I did not speak to your fathers or command them concerning burnt offerings and sacrifices' (Jer. 7:22). See also Ps 50:12–14. New Testament traces abound too: Mtt. 9:13; 12:7. Add to these, Stephen's speech, evoking the line of criticisms of the old cult and temple (Acts 7); Jesus' driving away of sellers from the temple, which Ratzinger construes as a symbolic depiction of the definitive casting out of the shadow and replacing it with reality.[21] Likewise, in the tearing of the temple veil at the moment of Jesus' death, the dawn of the new reality is witnessed as 'the prayer of the man Jesus is now united with the dialogue of eternal love within the Trinity. Jesus draws men into this prayer through the Eucharist, which is thus the ever – open door of adoration and the true Sacrifice, the Sacrifice of the New Covenant, "the reasonable service of God".'[22] Thus, the liturgical and self-revelatory trajectory of God's people finds its culmination.

The Primacy of Worship: *Sacrosanctum Concilium's* Corelation to *Lumen Gentium*

It is therefore a credit to Vatican II's determination to return to Sacred Scripture and Patristic habit of mind that it sought to reassert this centrality of authentic worship (the liturgy).Characteristically, Ratzinger interprets that the placing of the Constitution on the Sacred Liturgy at the beginning of the documents of Vatican II., even though it was 'basically due to pragmatic motives [...] has a deeper meaning within the

20   Cf. Ibid., 39.
21   Cf. Ibid., 41, 43.
22   Ibid., 48–49.

structure of the Council: adoration comes first. Therefore, God comes first.'[23] Pope Paul VI, in his closing address for the second session of the Council and the promulgation of *Sacrosanctum Concilium*, corroborates the primacy of God, and so of prayer. 'We may see in this', says the pope, 'an acknowledgment of a right order of values and duties: God in the first place; prayer our first duty; the liturgy the first school of spirituality, the first gift which we can bestow upon Christians who believe and pray with us. It is the first invitation to the world to break forth in happy and truthful prayer and to feel the ineffable life-giving force ....'[24] This, Ratzinger notes, 'corresponds to the norm of the Benedictine Rule: *Operi Dei nihil praeponatur* (Let nothing be placed before the work of God, the Divine Office)'.[25] Similarly, *Lumen Gentium*, the Constitution on the Church, follows the one on the liturgy, showing their correlation. In her work, *Ratzinger's Faith*, Tracey Rowland, a member of the International Theological Commission, and also a member of the editorial board of the English language edition of *Communio* (co-founded by Ratzinger) and winner of the 2020 Ratzinger Price, reflecting on Ratzinger's contribution and position on the theme of 'Liturgy since Vatican II', pertinently accentuates this correlation of the liturgy and the Church. She avers that '*Sacrosanctum concilium* reiterated that the liturgy is the embodiment of the Paschal Mystery, which is a mystery of worship, and consequently that the liturgy is intimately related to the mystery of the Church herself, that is, to her nuptial union with Christ.'[26] Correspondingly, too, the pastoral Constitution on the Church in the Modern World comes at the end of the Council documents to show the mission of the Church in bringing the whole creation, in response to God's call (*Dei Verbum*), back in adoration. It is worth citing Ratzinger at some length on this:

23   Ratzinger, *The Ecclesiology of the Constitution on the Church*, 5.
24   Pope Paul VI, Closing Address at the Second Session of Vatican II, 4 December 1963. Reprinted in Xavier Rynne, *The Second Session: The Debates and Decrees of Vatican II*, 29 September to 4 December 1963, 369.
25   Ratzinger, *The Ecclesiology of the Constitution on the Church*, 5.
26   T. Rowland, *Ratzinger's Faith: The Theology of Pope Benedict XVI* (New York: Oxford University Press, 2008), 123.

As the second text of the Council, the Constitution on the Church should be considered as inwardly connected with the text on the liturgy. The Church is guided by prayer, by the mission of glorifying God. By its nature, ecclesiology is connected with the liturgy. It is, therefore, logical that the third Constitution should speak of the Word of God that convokes the Church and renews her in every age. The fourth Constitution shows how the glorification of God is realized in the active life, since the light received from God is carried into the world and only in this way becomes fully the glorification of God.[27]

The ditching of this liturgical/ecclesial reality was, perhaps, the major post-conciliar catastrophe, in Ratzinger's view: 'The Constitution on the Liturgy was certainly no longer understood from the viewpoint of the basic primacy of adoration, but rather as a recipe book of what we can do with the Liturgy.'[28] In this climate of indiscriminate 'urgent' calls for, and attempts at, reform, 'the fact that the Liturgy is actually "made" for God and not for ourselves, seems to have escaped the minds of those who are busy pondering how to give the Liturgy an ever more attractive and communicable shape, actively involving an ever greater number of people.' Ironically, as he pertinently observes, the liturgy becomes less and less attractive the more we try to customize it for ourselves, as the essential focus on God is progressively lost.[29]

Ratzinger's Marian ecclesiology is a carefully considered attempt at restoring this lost focus. It reveals Mary as the ideal Church in prayer. She is a living liturgy. He notes how, 'by never mentioning Mary's name in his Gospel, Saint John wonderfully portrays Mary as the epitome and the arrival point of the true concept of prayer according to the Fathers of the Church, as being "a longing for God"'.[30] Ratzinger highlights the teaching of the Fathers of the Church that the true meaning of prayer is in fact 'becoming a longing for God' and underscores that Mary embodies not just this petition but its perfect answer. She is 'the open vessel of longing, in which life becomes prayer and prayer becomes life'.[31] She, as God's living Holy Soil, demonstrates

27 Ratzinger, *The Ecclesiology of the Constitution on the Church*, 5.
28 Ibid.
29 Ibid.
30 J. Ratzinger, 'My Word Shall Not Return to Me Empty', in H. U. von Balthasar and J. Ratzinger, *Mary: The Church*, 15.
31 Ibid. I have explored this further in *Mary, Daughter Zion*.

'how men can become fruitful soil for God's Word. They can become this soil by providing, as it were, the organic elements in which life can grow and mature; by drawing life themselves from this organic matter; by becoming themselves as a word formed by the penetration of the Word; by sinking the roots of their life into prayer and thus into God.'[32] Mary retains in this way an indisputable position both in the Church's daily life of devotion and in her official worship. (A liturgically based order like the Cistercians, for instance, dedicates all their churches to Mary.) She is 'above all the example of that worship that consists in making one's life an offering to God [...] as she, anticipating in herself the wonderful petition of the Lord's Prayer – "Your will be done" (Mt 6:10) – replied to God's messenger: "I am the handmaid of the Lord. Let what you have said be done to me" (Lk 1:38).'[33]

This focus may have been lost in the aftermath of the Council, yet common practice and the teaching office of the Church of both the West and East have never failed to recognize the relationship between Mary and the liturgy. She has long been seen – in the Tradition of the Church – 'as a model of the spiritual attitude with which the Church celebrates and lives the divine mysteries [...] a most excellent exemplar [...] of that interior disposition with which the Church, the beloved spouse, closely associated with her Lord, invokes Christ and through Him worships the eternal Father.'[34] In the Annunciation, in her Magnificat, in her pondering Jesus' words and the Christ events in heart, in her petition at Cana, and in her prayer with the disciples in the Upper Room, Mary is presented to us as the Church's model of prayer. Hence, as Paul VI notes, in her liturgy, the Church emulates Mary's part in the Incarnation and her meditation upon the events and mysteries of Christ's life, as 'with faith she listens, accepts, proclaims and venerates the word of God, distributes it to the faithful as the bread of life and in the light of that word examines the signs of the times and interprets and lives the events of history'.[35] Like Mary, the title 'virgin in prayer' is proper to the Church.[36]

32   Ibid., 14–15.
33   Pope Paul VI, *Marialis Cultus*, 21; Cf. Carroll, *Understanding the Mother of Jesus*, 26.
34   Pope Paul VI, *Marialis Cultus*, 16; Cf. *Sacrosanctum Concilium*, 7.
35   Ibid., 17.
36   Ibid., 18.

The Mass is, obviously, the central liturgical act of the Church, the crux of the Church's 'yes', just as the Cross was for Mary. There is a clear parallel between Christ's literal self-immolation and Mary's interior self-immolation and this parallel holds in the intimacy of her position under the dying body of her son. In the Mass, that mysterious episode of Mary, the other women, and the beloved disciple under the Cross, plays itself out anew. On the altar, the Marian mystery of compassionate *kenosis*[37] is once again experienced by the Church in her Eucharistic re-enactment of Calvary. Mary's self-immolation under the Cross, joined to that of her Son and Lord, is at the heart of the Eucharistic feast, as the Church surrenders completely to the 'Allness' of God's action in what Balthasar sees as 'Theo-drama'. The Mass becomes the place where the rupture in the relational being of the old Adam and the old Eve is rendered whole and holy again by the obedience of total surrender in the New Adam and the New Eve. This is represented on the Eucharistic altar as the image of the altar of our hearts, in the sacramental celebration of the *logikē latreia*. Thus, Ratzinger has good reason to say that the Mass is the Church's constitution.[38] For, in the Mass (just as it was for Mary under the Cross), the Church is fully herself; born, celebrated, taught and nourished.

Here, too, the Church's true identity is found,[39] in a way analogous to the Old Testament People of God. In their triple visits to the temple annually for the great feasts (Passover, Pentecost and the Feast of Tabernacles) they manifest themselves as 'God's pilgrim people, always journeying toward its God and receiving its identity and unity increasingly from the encounter with God in the one Temple'.[40] Essentially, the liturgy both constitutes and expresses the Church.[41] Citing Dalmais, Ambrosius Verheul argues that the liturgy 'is essentially an *expression*, a *manifestation*', the 'very action of the Church, the deed whereby the Church becomes actualized in the

---

37   Which we saw in *Mary, Daughter Zion*.

38   Cf. Ratzinger, *The Ecclesiology of Vatican II*, 5.

39   She is by her very nature constituted and lives by the Eucharist. Cf. Heim, *Joseph Ratzinger*, 518.

40   Ratzinger, *Jesus of Nazareth*, 121–122.

41   Cf. I. H. Dalmais, 'The Liturgy: "Action" of the Church', in P. J. Burns (ed.), *Mission and Witness: The Life of the Church* (London: Geoffrey Chapman, 1965), 355.

philosophic sense'. In the liturgy, he continues, 'she puts into operation the full riches of her inner being, experiences her own mystery in her action and reveals it to the outside world. In the liturgy the Church "realizes", in Newman's sense of that word, the fullness of her inner being; she becomes keenly conscious of her calling. The liturgy is the highest expression of the Church's life; it is an epiphany, a becoming visible of the Church. The liturgy activates the Church.'[42] In the ideal form of liturgical celebration, the true reality of the Church is experienced, not just 'in a scholastic sense' but, lived in the sense 'that we enter into it with the surrender of our whole person',[43] as Mary demonstrates. Allowing ourselves to be, in Verheul's words, completely 'assumed into the liturgy-celebrating community', we truly become and behold the authentic face of the Church.[44]

The deep connections between Mariology, ecclesiology and liturgy have significant mystagogical imports for Christian worship in Ratzinger's interpretation of the Church's liturgy. Firstly, the nature and meaning of the Church's liturgy are more readily disclosed if the person of Mary becomes a mirror for authentic liturgical pedagogy. Secondly, we have already noted the possible confusion regarding who actually is the New Temple, Christ or Mary? Thirdly, the question arises as to whether the *logos* sacrifice – this universal worship for all nations in spirit and truth[45] – inaugurated at the Annunciation, still needs an altar in time and place. And if so, what is Mary's relationship to the Christian altar?

42   A. Verheul, *Introduction to the Liturgy* (Wheathampstead: Anthony Clarke, 1972), 98.

43   Ibid.

44   Cf. Ibid.

45   Cf. Chapter 3. Its reality, proclaimed by Stephen, finds its details in that controversial pronouncement of Christ justifying his driving people away from the Temple as he cites the prophecy of Isaiah 56:7, 'these I shall lead to my holy mountain and make them joyful in my house of prayer. Their burnt offerings and sacrifices will be accepted on my altar, for my house will be called a house of prayer for all peoples' (Mk 11:17).

Liturgy as Theo-Drama / *Actio Divina*

We can begin by recalling Ratzinger's view that liturgy is the 'expression of the Church, to which the personal, what is one's own, has to surrender'.[46] That the Mass is the Church's constitution and essence is the core of Catholic Christianity. It may sound like an overstatement when Henri de Lubac states: 'Don't those who accept Jesus while rejecting his Church know that in the last analysis they have the Church to thank for him? [...] "Without the Church Christ would be bound to evaporate, crumble, become extinguished." And what would mankind be, were Christ to have been taken from them?'[47] I think that this needs to be read with an eye on the command 'Do this in remembrance of me' (Lk 22:19). Only then will it become clear how the Eucharist (that which is the 'source and summit'[48] of all the Church is and does), is central to Christianity. Here, too, we see why Ratzinger insists that the only thing that really counts in the Church is that which is not *ours*.[49] The source of the Church's pride is also the reason for her humility. This is because, true to his Marian ecclesiology, Ratzinger sees the liturgy as a rite in which the principal protagonist is God. It is a theo-drama or *action divina* (God's action). This understanding, one could say, is the hinge on which hang all his liturgical emphases.[50]

But there is another vital ingredient. The idea of 'play' relative to the liturgy, as originally conceived by Guardini, can perhaps be called the landmark in the book *The Spirit of the Liturgy*,[51] which is the seminal work of this great mentor of Ratzinger. For Guardini, liturgy is, properly so called,

---

46   Heim, *Joseph Ratzinger*, 518.

47   H. De. Lubac, cited in J. Ratzinger, 'Why I Am Still in the Church', in H. U. von Balthasar and J. Ratzinger (eds), *Two Say Why*, 81–82.

48   Cf. CCC 1324; LG 11.

49   J. Ratzinger, 'Why I Am Still in the Church', in H. U. von Balthasar and J. Ratzinger (eds), *Two Say Why*, 79.

50   This is evident in his main works on the liturgy. Cf. Ratzinger, *The Spirit of the Liturgy*; Ratzinger, *Feast of Faith*.

51   R. Guardini, *The Spirit of the Liturgy* (Brescia: Morcelliana, 1980).

a play, a divinely ordained game to be played in liberty and beauty and holy joy before God. It exists not for the sake of humanity, but for the sake of God.[52] He gives this stand a Scriptural grounding, tracing it right from the mysteries of the eternal beginning, that eternal play of the Son before the Father (Pr 8:30), devoid of any 'purpose' except that simple fact, that the Son 'plays' happily before the Father.[53] Hence, the liturgy makes us childlike, transforming us into works of art before God, playing just as David danced before the ark. It is easy to see how such pure and trustful surrender engenders a transforming conformity to, and union with, the *Logos* as it makes us docile and pliable which, yet again, is the proper hermeneutic of the 'yes' of Mary. Indeed, Ratzinger explains how we are so drawn into Christ's worship that *actio Christi* becomes our action too.[54] This 'Playfulness of the Liturgy' is one of Guardini's remarkable legacies. His exposition of the objectivity, impersonality and fellowship of the liturgical prayer together with its style, symbolism and seriousness, all draw their strength from this basic understanding of liturgy as Theo-drama.[55] As the nomenclature deliberately suggests, Ratzinger's *The Spirit of the Liturgy* has much in common with this basic thought of Guardini. Ratzinger acknowledges as much in his preface.[56] Guardini's book, he argues, made a

52   Ibid., 32.
53   Discussing 'The Playfulness of the Liturgy', in Chapter 5, Guardini also alludes to the 'aimless' play of the angels in Ezekiel's vision. Amazingly he finds his way reasonably dragging this idea to the end, to that eschatological play of 'purposeless' and 'timeless', eternal worship of God. And he warns those who reject this understanding of liturgy of being scandalized in the end to discover '… that the heavenly consummation is an eternal song of praise'.
54   'The point is that, ultimately, the difference between the actio Christi and our own action is done away with. There is only one action, which is at the same time his and ours – ours because we have become "one body and one spirit" with him. The uniqueness of the Eucharistic liturgy lies precisely in the fact that God himself is acting and that we are drawn into that action of God.' J. Ratzinger, *The Spirit of the Liturgy*, 174.
55   Cf. Guardini, *The Spirit of the Liturgy*.
56   There he states: 'One of my first readings after the beginning of my theological studies, at the beginning of 1946, was Romano Guardini's little book "The Spirit of the Liturgy", published at Easter of 1918.' Ratzinger, *The Spirit of the Liturgy*, 7–8.

decisive contribution to the rediscovery of the liturgy as the vital centre of the Church and Christian life. His own book has similar intent: 'My purpose in writing this little book', he says, '... is to assist this renewal of understanding. Its basic intentions coincide with what Guardini wanted to achieve in his own time with *The Spirit of the Liturgy*. That is why I deliberately chose a title that would be immediately reminiscent of that classic of liturgical theology.'[57]

As earlier noted, an overriding idea in Ratzinger's book is the 'sole' agency of God, and so, God-centredness, in the liturgy as *actio divina*. If worship is, and should always be, God-centred as Mary is, then Ratzinger is led to distrust the common understanding of that active participation (*actuosa* not *activa* in fact) recommended by the Council. Here, he is in full accord with Saint John Paul's teaching. *Actuosa participatio* does not simply mean activism; everyone singing together, for instance. Rather, he argues that listening to a choir perform sacred music during Mass, is full participation. He gives us a masterly account of what participation, not only of man, but of the entire creation, really signifies: 'What happens in it is that the human actio [...] steps back and makes way for the actio divina, the action of God.'[58] On the eucharistic altar, this action of God is effected through the *oratio*, in human speech. For Ratzinger, this is 'the real "action" for which all of creation is in expectation'. He is at his best in his couching of this action: 'The elements of the earth are transubstantiated, pulled, so to speak, from their creaturely anchorage, grasped at the deepest ground of their being, and changed into the Body and Blood of the Lord.'[59]

Ratzinger's understanding of Catholic worship proceeds from this basic idea of the liturgy as principally *actio divina*, something received, just as Scripture and Tradition are. Thus, no one, not even the Roman Pontiff, who according to him, 'can only be a humble servant of its lawful development and abiding integrity and identity'[60] has authority to alter the essence of the liturgy, even though, of course, an organic development of its expression through time may occur. This is because the liturgy's meaning

57 Ibid., 7–8. What Guardini began, finds its flowering in Ratzinger.
58 Ibid., 172.
59 Ibid., 173.
60 Ibid., 166.

and fundamental form have been directly determined by God through his actions in the history of his people, and not through 'human innovation or genius'. The agitations of the liturgical movements for and against reform in the liturgy find a coherent answer in Ratzinger's understanding of the liturgy. The understanding of liturgy as primarily an act of God, whose very history must be received as gift, speaks to those whose focus is always on innovations and change. Similarly, for those over-zealous for an 'active participation' which misinterprets *participatio actuosa* as 'activity', Ratzinger says: 'Doing must really stop when we come to the heart of the matter: the oratio. It must be plainly evident that the oratio is the heart of the matter, but that it is important precisely because it provides a space for the actio of God .... The almost theatrical entrance of different players into the liturgy, which is so common today, quite simply misses the point. If the liturgy degenerates into general activity, then we have radically misunderstood the "theo-drama" of the liturgy and lapsed almost into parody.'[61] The history of salvation records the progressive transformation of the ancient notion that 'worship involves a circular movement of giving and receiving' between the gods and man. This circular movement, in 'two parts: the power of the gods supporting the world, but also the gift of man, which provides for the gods', gives the impression of mutual dependence between God and man.[62] From the story of creation, through the foreshadowing of the sole agency of God in the sacrifice of the Lamb on Calvary, in the divinely provided lamb of Abraham's sacrifice (Gen. 22:12–14), and the requisite deference to divine volition on mount Sinai (Exod. 32), the essence of worship as theo-drama is established.

Purposeful and differentiated activity is taken, especially in the modern world, to be more 'serious' than play. But Ratzinger does not agree. For him, play is a major component, 'an authentic element of our existence'.[63] Hence, the modern 'Iscariotan' and masculine mentality that contests the 'wastage' at the feet of Jesus (Jn 12:4) are blind both to the nature of human existence and to true worship. The same mentality may see nothing wrong

61   Ibid., 174–175.
62   Ibid., 25.
63   Ratzinger and Seewald, *Salt of the Earth*, 69.

in diverting resources to self-willed projects (Jn 12:6). It is a tendency towards the false divinization of Man that places him in the lead even in the liturgy, which should only be based on a Marian receptivity – a fruitful space, an awaiting soil, for the action of God.

For Ratzinger, the worship of the golden calf in Exodus is the antithesis of this Marian-liturgical profile.[64] There, the people resisted 'wasting time' in waiting for, and following of, God's own rubrics, but instead fashioned their own liturgy and their own god, which, of course, became their creature. Ratzinger warns against the dangers in this attitude: 'Worship becomes a feast that the community gives itself, a festival of self-affirmation. Instead of being the worship of God, it becomes a circle closed in on itself: eating, drinking, and making merry. The dance around the golden calf is the image of this self-seeking worship. It is a kind of banal self-gratification. The narrative of the golden calf is a warning about any kind of self-initiated and self-seeking worship.'[65]

This Marian lesson is, of course, not limited to the liturgy, but extends to man's social life, which is meant to flow from the authentic Christian understanding of Man, realized in our participation in the *actio divina*. Hence, Ratzinger's neat formula: 'orthodoxy is inward "orthopraxis"'[66] which is also true when reversed, since our actions ought to be an expression of our true adoration. 'For the shape of Christian worship reproduces, at the same time, *both the way to go and the manner of going in human life.*'[67] Here the words of the Council Fathers in *Gaudium et Spes*[68] corroborates Guardini's belief, as expressed in his fifth chapter on *The Playfulness of the Liturgy*, that, in the liturgy, man is granted the opportunity, enabled by grace, to realize his fundamental essence, to become that which he is called to be – a personification of, and living response to *actio divina*.

---

64   Cf. Ratzinger, *The Spirit of the Liturgy*, 23.
65   Ibid.
66   Ibid., 160.
67   J. Ratzinger, 'The Church Subsists as Liturgy', in S. O. Horn and V. Pfnür (eds), *God Is Near Us*, 122.
68   'The truth is that only in the mystery of the incarnate Word does the mystery of man take on light.' GS 22.

Logikē Latreia: The Church as God's Temple

This Marian-liturgical profile raises the question of Mary's relationship with the Temple. If the temple bears in shadow the Presence of God, does she not do the same in reality? Is she then the New Temple? Ratzinger is always careful to avoid this identification which is contrary to Christ's own words. One instance can be given where he uses the same appellation for both. On the effects of the 'yes' of Mary, he holds that, on the part of God, 'Mary's Yes opens to him the space wherein he can pitch his tent. She herself becomes his tent.'[69] Yet in another text he says: 'The annunciation of Mary happens to a woman, in an insignificant town .... Thus begins a new way, at whose centre stands no longer the temple, but the simplicity of Jesus Christ. He is now the true temple, the tent of meeting'.[70] Christ and Mary appear to be described by the same parlance, sharing the same title. This is an anxiety that attends all Mariology. *Lumen Gentium*, and Paul VI's *Marialis Cultus*, is particularly attentive to it,[71] but more can be said.

69   J. Ratzinger, 'Et Incarnatus est de Spiritu Sancto ex Maria Virgine', in H. U. von Balthasar and J. Ratzinger, *Mary: The Church*, 93–94.

70   Ratzinger, *Daughter Zion*, 42.

71   See for instance, LG 60–65. Also, number 57 of *Marialis Cultus*, notes: 'Christ is the only way to the Father (cf. Jn 14:4–11), and the ultimate example to whom the disciple must conform his own conduct (cf. Jn 13:15), to the extent of sharing Christ's sentiments (cf. Ph 2:5), living His life and possessing His Spirit (cf. Ga 2: 20; Rm 8:10–11). The Church has always taught this and nothing in pastoral activity should obscure this doctrine. But the Church, taught by the Holy Spirit and benefiting from centuries of experience, recognizes that devotion to the Blessed Virgin, subordinated to worship of the divine Savior and in connection with it, also has a great pastoral effectiveness and constitutes a force for renewing Christian living. It is easy to see the reason for this effectiveness Mary's many-sided mission to the People of God is a super natural reality which operates and bears fruit within the body of the Church.' 'In the Virgin Mary everything is relative to Christ and dependent upon Him .... according to the perennial mind of the Church ... "what is given to the handmaid is referred to the Lord; thus what is given to the Mother redounds to the Son; ... and thus what is given as humble tribute to the Queen becomes honor rendered to the King".' Pope Paul VI, *Marialis Cultus*, 25.

In the first place, Mary is not in the strict sense the Temple, but could be seen as the living Ark of the Covenant.[72] Ratzinger notes that: 'Even early traditions portray God as dwelling "in the womb" of Israel – in the Ark of the Covenant. This dwelling "in the womb" of Israel now becomes quite literally real in the virgin of Nazareth. Mary herself becomes the true Ark of the Covenant in Israel so that the symbol of the Ark gathers an incredible realistic force: God in the flesh of a human being, which flesh now becomes his dwelling place in the midst of creation.'[73]

Secondly, the use of the definite article before 'temple' introduces a difference and specification. One could interpret Ratzinger as meaning that whereas Christ is the true temple and the tent of meeting, Mary is God's temple, God's tent. She is the model of that which we are all called to be, even though she is that in a primordial and eminent degree. Christ is the new and literal temple – his body replaces the temple as presence of God and place of worship – Mary is a sign of this since she bears the presence of God within her and she is an exemplar of how, as St Paul argues, the bodies of all Christians are the temple of the Holy Spirit. It is true that elsewhere Ratzinger uses the article also for Mary saying: 'Just as Mary was depicted earlier as the new Israel, the true "daughter of Zion", so now she appears as the temple upon which descends the cloud in which God walks into the midst of history.'[74] Here it is clear that the referent is not Christ but Mary as the temple of the Incarnation. It is significant how Ratzinger here presents Mary's image as the temple, as not a matter of taking and asserting a position, but of making way for the Lord. For he concludes: 'Whoever puts himself at God's disposal disappears with him in the cloud, into oblivion and insignificance, and precisely in this way acquires a share in his glory.'[75] Thus, the conflict or competition that naturally arises regarding who actually is the temple is attended to by the very disposition of surrender in the 'yes'.

72   Cf. J. Ratzinger, 'Et Incarnatus est de Spiritu Sancto ex Maria Virgine', in H. U. von Balthasar and J. Ratzinger, *Mary: The Church*, 87–88.
73   Ibid., 65.
74   Ratzinger, *Introduction to Christianity*, 273.
75   Ibid.

In a similar way, when he writes about the symbolism of water in the Gospel of John (which he sees as pointing to the Christ – the temple from whom the life-giving water flowed) Ratzinger notes how the same could and does apply to the believer as well: 'The application ... primarily to Christ ... does not have to exclude a secondary interpretation referring to the believer. A saying from the apocryphal Gospel of Thomas (108) points in a similar direction to John's Gospel: "Whoever drinks from my mouth shall become as I am" .... The believer becomes one with Christ and participates in his fruitfulness. The man who believes and loves with Christ becomes a well that gives life.'[76] If Christians are God's temple (1 Cor 3:16,17; 6:19; 2 Cor 6:16; Eph 2:21; 1 Pt 2:5), then that possibility had its inauguration in Mary's sacrificial 'yes'. In this, subsequent to it and consequent upon it, the Church becomes a spiritual temple, not made by human hands. Hence, Isaac of Stella notes: 'This is why Scripture says: I will dwell in the inheritance of the Lord. The Lord's inheritance is, in a general sense, the Church; in a special sense, Mary; in an individual sense, the Christian. Christ dwelt for nine months in the tabernacle of Mary's womb. He dwells until the end of the ages in the tabernacle of the Church's faith. He will dwell forever in the knowledge and love of each faithful soul.'[77] There is a sense in which 'the temple' applies both to Mary and to Christ but Ratzinger insists there is only one authentic sacrifice – that sacrifice of the *Logos* himself. The Church as individuals and collectively are invited to unite with this one sacrifice, conforming to the *Logos*, and so becoming one with him.

Though there is a real sense in which Mary can be seen as the temple, yet there is only one temple – Christ – every other is a temple only by participation in, or in union with that one Temple. Ratzinger is clear on this: 'The man Jesus is the dwelling-place of the Word, the eternal divine Word, in this world. Jesus' "flesh", his human existence, is the "dwelling" or "tent" of the Word: the reference to the sacred tent of Israel in the wilderness is unmistakable. Jesus is, so to speak, the "tent" of meeting – he is the reality for which the tent and the later Temple could only serve as signs.'[78] Yet there is no competition here.

76   Ratzinger, *Jesus of Nazareth*, I, 248.
77   Isaac of Stella, *Mary and the Church*, 94–96.
78   Ratzinger, *Jesus of Nazareth*, 11.

We can put it like this. The same relationship between the 'yes' of Christ and Mary's 'yes' somehow overflows to this. Just as the 'yes' of Mary, representative of the Church's, was only a human complement to the 'yes' of Christ, and as grace becomes truly grace only with its complement, so is Mary, and the Church in her, incorporated into the temple which is Christ. This fits into the logic of the Incarnation and of the Church as the mystical body of Christ. Christ is the temple as head and members. Our participation in him as the body and its head, also defines our participation in him as the Temple. And this is primordially, pre-eminently and representatively realized in the 'yes' of Mary which is implicit in her Immaculate Conception and explicit in the Annunciation.

The New Temple (of the Universal 'Logos Worship') and the Christian Altar

Further problems present themselves here. The Epistle to the Hebrews, for instance, seems to suggest that the only sacrifice Christians should now make is through 'good works': 'So Jesus also suffered outside the gate in order to sanctify the people through his own blood. Therefore, let us go forth to him outside the camp and bear the abuse he endured [...] Through him then let us continually offer up a sacrifice of praise to God, that is, the fruit of lips that acknowledge his name. Do not neglect to do good and to share what you have, for such sacrifices are pleasing to God' (Heb 13:12–13). Furthermore, Revelation 21:22 declares that the New Jerusalem needs no temple because Almighty God and the Lamb are themselves its Temple. So, do we still need altars? Ratzinger draws attention to the 'not yet' that is part of the Christian existence, for the New Heaven and the New Earth have not already come. Here he echoes Oscar Cullman's formulation in noting that, in relation to the fullness of our salvation and of the coming of God's kingdom, there is a mixture of 'already and not yet'.[79] Hence, we still need sacred space, sacred time

79   Cf. Ibid., 54.

and mediating symbols despite the prophetic denunciations of external worship, the tearing of the temple veil and the opening of the heart of God in the pierced heart of the Crucified. Ratzinger is very precise here, saying: 'Yes we do need them precisely so that, through the "image", through the sign, we learn to see the openness of heaven.' We need them particularly because our spiritual participation in the heavenly liturgy is necessarily 'mediated to us through earthly signs, which the Redeemer has shown to us as the place where his reality is to be found'.[80] Through the pierced body of Christ, the perpetually torn veil that unlocked heaven, rendered present in the liturgy, the earth reaches to heaven and gap is bridged.[81] This, no doubt, is again founded on and guaranteed by the same logic of the Incarnation, which Ratzinger sees as the full real-ization of the sacrifice of the *Logos*. Though 'God is spiritual and God is everywhere [...] Just as God assumed a body and entered the time and space of this world, so it is appropriate to prayer – at least to communal li-turgical prayer – that our speaking to God should be "incarnational", that it should be Christological, turned through the incarnate Word to the triune God.'[82] We recall here Ratzinger's view of the *Primacy of the Logos* which I explored considerably in *Mary, Daughter Zion*, the highlight of which is the incarnation of the Logos. The Logos is a person and thus the universal and the particular coincide. In the revelation of the *Logos Incarnatus*, the particular is not swallowed up in the universal. Rather, the particular not only retains its existence but commands primacy. And neither does the primacy of the particular mean the abolition of plurality. It is indeed its affirmation.[83] Hence, Christian altars are neither rendered

80   Ibid., 61.
81   Ratzinger comments: 'The Eucharist is an entry into the liturgy of heaven; by it we become contemporaries with Jesus Christ's own act of worship, into which, through his Body, he takes up worldly time and straightaway leads it beyond itself.' Ratzinger, *Spirit of the Liturgy*, 70; 'Heaven has been opened up by the union of the man Jesus, and thus all human existence, with the living God. But this new open-ness is only mediated by the signs of salvation. We need mediation. As yet we do not see the Lord "as he is".' Ibid., 60.
82   Ibid., 75–76.
83   *Mary, Daughter Zion*, Chapter 1.

obsolete, nor illogical, by the new reality of the spiritual, universal worship, the *logikē latreia*. They are its true expression.

Ratzinger's exposition is not primarily concerned with the abolition of the old temple, but the establishment of the new temple in Christ, realized especially at the Incarnation and the altar of the Cross, the paschal altar where Ratzinger locates the risen body of Christ. His contention is that the new single temple of Christ's body does not make myriad Christian altars pointless but is temporally realized in them following the same mystery of the 'already and not yet' fundamental to eschatological understanding of time, the distinction between realized and unrealized eschatology – the one containing the other. Here, time completes in itself the past, and lives in anticipation of the future, while still in pilgrimage towards it. That is exactly what is realized on the Eucharistic altar; where the past is represented and the future is anticipated in a present mystical openness to eschatology.[84] Thus Ratzinger remarks: 'In virtue of Jesus' Cross and Resurrection, the Eucharist is the meeting point of all the lines that lead from the Old Covenant, indeed from the whole of man's religious history.' 'Here at last', he concludes, 'is right worship, ever longed for and surpassing our powers: adoration "in spirit and truth".'[85]

In this way, the Marian line, the Marian mystery, which we have so far traced from the Old Testament through the New to the Church's teachings and theological reflections, also finds its arrival point in the Eucharistic mystery. Mary, as God's temple, in and through Christ, is crucial to a proper understanding of the Eucharist. Mary is in, and indeed is, the Church that celebrates the Eucharist, and so definitely has her place in the Church's liturgy.

In and through Christ, the new sacrifice is completed, yet the same sacrifice is perennially present in the Church. Though, for Ratzinger, liturgy is 'the worship of an open heaven'[86] – one could say that it is a realization of our baptismal status as God's temple (as exemplified in the open heaven at the baptism of the Lord) – the Christian altar is still central in

---

84 Cf. CCC 1402; SC 47.
85 Ratzinger, *The Spirit of the Liturgy*, 47.
86 Ibid., 49.

that worship. Ratzinger's reflection here is not anti-cultic. We need to read him in more detail to see how 'the worship of an open heaven' forms part of his more developed position on the liturgy. His exposition intimates an ideal of what a theology of the temple or Christian altar ought to be and how this is revealed even in the 'yes' of Mary. It exemplifies the guidelines for a theology of the altar given by one of the contributors at the Bose International theological Convention[87] in that it is not a criticism of cult as such, not an abstract approach inspired by systematic theology nor clamour for change in accordance with socio-cultural conditions and pragmatic liturgical activism. It is biblical, dogmatic, moral, typological and analogical in an integral whole. It is astonishing how Ratzinger connects every segment of faith and theology together, insofar as they proceed and cohere from the 'yes' of Mary enfolded in the 'yes' of Christ. The unity and coherence of his vision is as remarkable as its depth.

The Place of Mary on the Christian Altar

One more question needs to be addressed. If Mary is truly the icon and type of the Church,[88] or indeed the Church in person, the spouse of the Lord, and the first Church on whose altar the *logos* sacrifice was first and fundamentally offered, what is her connection with the altars in Catholic churches and the liturgy directed towards them?

Ratzinger's thoughts on the 'yes' of Mary, and the Church, to the Incarnate Word are immensely helpful here for we have to navigate between opposed tendencies whose force must be admitted. Ratzinger agrees with Balthasar. He says: 'If the Son is truly incarnate this event really reaches into the "flesh" and, inversely, because man is one and entire, the "flesh" reaches into the personal centre of the Logos.'[89] This insight addresses any

87 A. Gerhards, 'Teologia dell'altare', in G. Boselli (ed.), *L'altare: mistero di presenza, opera dell' arte* (Magnano: edizioni Qiqajon, 2005), 213–232.
88 LG 63.
89 Ratzinger, *Daughter Zion*, 49.

scrupulous fear that the introduction of the human and historical into divine worship would defile the pure divinity of God. This, in Ratzinger's view, negates the reality of the Incarnation. It is based on an erroneous purism and goes against the discernment principle of 1 John 4:2.[90] The truth that 'the flesh reaches to the personal centre of the Logos' is an important part of Ratzinger's thought. This human flesh derives from Mary, his mother, and does so in time and for eternity. Hence, he praises the Catholicism of his native Bavaria, which, according to him, 'knew how to provide room for all that was human, both prayer and festivities, penance and joy. A joyful, colourful, human Christianity', as against a purist or overly idealistic mentality.[91] He therefore cautions: 'We cannot try to bypass these human faces in order to get to God alone, in his "pure form", as it were. This would lead us to a God of our own invention in place of the real God; it would be an arrogant purism that regards its own ideas as more important than God's deeds .... Mary is one of the human beings who in an altogether special way belong[s] to the name of God, so much so, in fact, that we cannot praise him rightly if we leave her out of account.'[92] Hence, at the centre of the 'oratio', the *logos* sacrifice, and its altar, is not an abstract and 'purely divine' Christ, but the Risen Body of the Crucified with the entire Christ event (through which our contact with God is effected) and all the components of that historicity, in which Mary's place cannot be insignificant. This is what the Eucharistic altar should, and does, represent. If Mary is located at the manifestation of the new temple inaugurated at the Annunciation and Incarnation, this immediately says something regarding what her place ought to be in the Eucharistic altar and in the liturgy.[93] Thus, the Council Fathers were right in admonishing

90   'Every spirit which acknowledges that Jesus the Christ has come in the flesh is from God' (1 Jn 4:2).

91   Cf. Ratzinger and Messori, *The Ratzinger Report*, 166.

92   J. Ratzinger, 'Hail Full of Grace', in H. U. von Balthasar and J. Ratzinger, *Mary: The Church*, 63.

93   'The examination of the revised liturgical books leads us to the comforting observation that the post-conciliar renewal has, as was previously desired by the liturgical movement, properly considered the Blessed Virgin in the mystery of Christ, and, in harmony with tradition, has recognized the singular place that belongs to her

'all the sons of the Church that the cult, especially the liturgical cult, of the Blessed Virgin, be generously fostered'.[94] Paul VI's *Marialis Cultus* asserts that the new Roman Missal, like Eastern liturgies which have always had more invocation of Mary built into them, demonstrates this.[95]

Ratzinger defends the use of images on the altar in a similar way. They are not distractions from true worship, for 'the image is at the service of the liturgy'.[96] This is because 'they open up the realism of the mystery without diverging from it. As for the mass, as the making present of the Cross, do these images not enable us to understand that mystery with a new vividness? [...] What power of inward devotion lies in the images of the Mother of God! They manifest the new humanity of the faith. Such images are an invitation to prayer, because they are permeated with prayer from within. They show us the true image of man as planned by the Creator and redeemed by Christ. They guide us into man's authentic being.'[97]

The Western Church has for the past thousand years privileged statues over and against icons. But Ratzinger's thinking is in deep accord with the theology developed round the latter. Evdokimov, for instance, explains how the icon is 'integrated into the liturgical mystery' as a sacramental reality, much in line with the concepts of *actio divina* and *theo-drama*, which we

---

in Christian worship as the holy Mother of God and the worthy Associate of the Redeemer.' Cf. Pope Paul VI, *Marialis Cultus*, 15.

94   LG 67.

95   'In the first place, we are pleased to note how the Eucharistic Prayers of the Missal, in admirable harmony with the Eastern liturgies (24) contain a significant commemoration of the Blessed Virgin. For example, the ancient Roman Canon, which commemorates the Mother of the Lord in terms full of doctrine and devotional inspiration: "In union with the whole Church we honor Mary, the ever-virgin Mother of Jesus Christ our Lord and God." In a similar way the recent Eucharistic Prayer III expresses with intense supplication the desire of those praying to share with the Mother the inheritance of sons: "May he make us an everlasting gift to you (the Father) and enable us to share in the inheritance of your saints, with Mary, the Virgin Mother of God." This daily commemoration, by reason of its place at the heart of the divine Sacrifice, should be considered a particularly expressive form of the veneration that the Church pays to the "Blessed of the Most High" (cf. Lk 1:28).' Pope Paul VI, *Marialis Cultus*, 10.

96   Ratzinger, *The Spirit of the Liturgy*, 133.

97   Ibid., 128.

have already discussed. It stands for something infinitely beyond itself. In it, 'we see a visualization, an imaged representation of the whole economy of salvation'.[98] The icon makes present, a 'living personal content', such that 'prayerful contemplation passes through the icon, so to speak, and does not stop until it reaches the living content, that is, the person represented'.[99] For, as the Seventh Ecumenical Council states, 'whether it be by the contemplation of the Scriptures or by the representation of the icon … we remember all the prototypes and we are introduced into their presence'.[100] In Mary's case, her image, not only opens up for us the infinite horizon of the mystery of the divine, but also places before the Church her (the Church's) true self, in order to achieve that self-knowledge and full presence necessary for proper worship.

The 'Gate of the East' and the Orientation of Christian Prayer

Ratzinger is a strong advocate of the East as the proper direction for liturgical prayer. This has displaced orientation towards Jerusalem, he argues, because the destroyed temple is overtaken as the place of God's earthly presence: 'The Temple built on stone has ceased to express the hope of Christians; its curtain is torn forever. Christians look towards the east, the rising sun.'[101] He says, in a reflection upon Psalm 19: 'Christians interpret it in terms of Christ, who is the living Word, the eternal Logos and thus the true light of history, who came forth in Bethlehem from the bridal chamber of the Virgin Mother and now pours out his light on all the world. The east supersedes Jerusalem Temple as a symbol. Christ, represented by the sun, is the place of the shekinah, the true throne of the living God. In the Incarnation, the human nature truly becomes the throne and seat of God, who is thus forever bound to the earth and accessible to our

98   Evdokimov, *The Art of the Icon*, 176.
99   Ibid., 175.
100   Cited by Evdokimov, ibid., 178.
101   Ratzinger, *The Spirit of the Liturgy*, 68.

prayers.'[102] This informs his view of the Christian altar, that 'the altar signifies the entry of him who is the Orient into the assembled community and the going out of the community from the prison of this world through the curtain now torn open'.[103] It is 'a participation in the pasch, the "passing over" from the world to God, which Christ has opened up'.[104] Prayer facing the east implies a Christology defined eschatologically, since it means going to meet the coming Christ and spells hope by pointing to the future, the New Heaven and the New Earth.[105] He accepts, however, that 'where a direct common turning towards the east is not possible, the cross can serve as the interior "east" of faith'.[106]

Here, again, Ratzinger situates the actualization in time of the coming of the Lord from the East on the 'the bridal chamber of the Virgin Mother' at the Incarnation. Later, as Pope Benedict XVI, he would call her '*Ianua Caeli*, Gate of Heaven'.[107] This is not strange to Scripture and Tradition. Coptic Orthodox authors take this further by surnaming Mary 'Gate of the East', following Ezekiel's prophecies, especially in Ezk 44:1–2 and Ezk 43:2–5. Patriarch Shenuoda III embraces the exegetical tradition of interpreting these texts as symbolizing 'the virginity of the Virgin who was from the countries of the East; and how this virginity remained sealed', and so, qualifies her as 'the gate of life' and 'the gate of deliverance'.[108] Interestingly, these are tittles which, according to his interpretation of Genesis 28: 17 ('"How awesome is this place! This is none other than the house of God, and this is the gate of heaven."'), Mary shares with the church.[109] Therefore, even

---

102 Ibid.
103 Ibid., 70.
104 Ibid.
105 Ibid., 69.
106 Ibid., 83.
107 Pope Benedict XVI, 'Angelus Address, 26th August 2007', in: <http://www.vatican.va/content/benedict-xvi/en/angelus/2007/documents/hf_ben-xvi_ang_20070826.html> (Accessed: 21 February 2021).
108 Cf. Patriarch Shenuoda III, *The Holy Virgin St. Mary*, Transl. from the Arabic edition of 1999, in: <https://st-takla.org/Feastes-&-Special-Events/Virgin-Mary-Fast/Saint-Mary-Fast_Virgin-Life-Hymns-mp3s-02-Pope-Shenouda-Virgin-Mary-Book.html> (Accessed: 22 February 2021).
109 Ibid.

in Ratzinger's celebrated facing the East or *conversi ad Dominum*,[110] as he often calls it, the figure of Mary is not absent. And, as Paul VI teaches, 'It could not have been otherwise. If one studies the history of Christian worship, in fact, one notes that both in the East and in the West the highest and purest expressions of devotion to the Blessed Virgin have sprung from the liturgy or have been incorporated into it.'[111]

Ratzinger's emphasis on facing the east is, as we might expect, linked with his other insights. Altar, orientation and cross are all connected, for 'Facing east … was linked with the "sign of the Son of Man", with the cross which announces the Lord's Second Coming. That is why very early on the east was linked with the sign of the Cross. Where a direct common turning toward the east is not possible, the cross can serve as the interior "east" of faith. It should stand in the middle of the altar and be the common point of focus for both priest and praying community.'[112]

This is very much in line with Ratzinger's position on the issue of whether the Eucharist is just a meal or sacrifice. It is a position he defends with great passion: 'True the Lord established the new reality of Christian worship within the framework of a Jewish (Passover) meal, but it was precisely this new reality, not the meal as such, that he commanded us to repeat.'[113] The Eucharist, according to him, 'refers back to the Cross and thus to the transformation of Temple sacrifice into worship of God that is in harmony with *logos*'.[114] 'On the altar' he says, 'what the Temple had in the past foreshadowed is now present in a new way. Yes, it enables us to become contemporaries of the Sacrifice of the Logos.'[115] Thus '… the synagogue liturgy of the Word, renewed and deepened in a Christian way, merged with the remembrance of Christ's death and Resurrection to become the "Eucharist", and precisely thus was fidelity to the command "Do this" fulfilled. This new and all-encompassing form of worship could

---

110 Ratzinger, *The Spirit of the Liturgy*, 72, 83.
111 Pope Paul VI, *Marialis Cultus*, 15.
112 Ratzinger, *The Spirit of the Liturgy*, 83.
113 Ibid., 78.
114 Ibid.
115 Ibid., 71.

not be derived simply from the meal ....'[116] It is pertinent to observe that it is the contrary position, rejected by Ratzinger, that makes the image either of the Cross or of Mary appear strange to the Christian altar. If the Christian altar is understood in the true light, as expressed by Ratzinger, and as we have briefly seen, the point of view will be different. Mary would find her place in the liturgy, just as she did beneath the Cross and at the Cana scene which anticipated it, as *Marialis Cultus* underscores.[117]

116   Ibid., 78–79.
117   'This union of the Mother and the Son in the work of redemption reaches its climax on Calvary, where Christ "offered himself as the perfect sacrifice to God" (Heb 9:14) and where Mary stood by the cross (cf. Jn 19:25), suffering grievously with her only-begotten Son. There she united herself with a maternal heart to His sacrifice, and lovingly consented to the immolation of this victim which she herself had brought forth "and also was offering to the eternal Father". To perpetuate down the centuries the Sacrifice of the Cross, the divine Savior instituted the Eucharistic sacrifice, the memorial of His death and resurrection, and entrusted it to His spouse the Church, which, especially on Sundays, calls the faithful together to celebrate the Passover of the Lord until He comes again. This the Church does in union with the saints in heaven and in particular with the Blessed Virgin, whose burning charity and unshakable faith she imitates.' Pope Paul VI, *Marialis Cultus*, 20.

CHAPTER 6

The Marian Church: Mission and Ministry

Mission and Ministry as Ecclesial Kenosis

The Mass is conducted at the altar but, as *Missa*, we are *sent* out from it into the world. This missionary nature of the Church significantly came to the fore in Vatican II Council. Ratzinger understands it in this way: 'The Council wanted to mark the transition from a protective to a missionary attitude. Many forget that for the Council the counter-concept to "conservative" is not "progressive" but "missionary".'[1] The premise of the document on the Church's missionary activity, *Ad Gentes*, is that the Church is 'divinely sent to the nations of the world to be unto them "a universal sacrament of salvation"'.[2] Mission is within the essence of the Church. Her progress can only be missionary. It can only be an increasing fruitfulness in responding to the bidding of her Lord. In holding that the constitution of the Church, indeed her very essence, is the Mass, Ratzinger brings together the nature of the Church and her mission, and what ministry in the Church ought to be. When she is designated as a Mass, from the Latin etymology *missa* (sent out), one reads already the sense of mission. However, Ratzinger adds that this implies 'a service of God, and therefore a service of man and a service for the transformation of the world'.[3] Thus, within this denomination of the Church's being and mission is contained also the indication of the ministerial ideal in the Church. Therefore, the image of the liturgy described above applies also to the mission of the Church and so dictates the exercise of her ministry.

1   Ratzinger and Messori, *The Ratzinger Report*, 13.
2   AG 1; Cf. LG 48.
3   Ratzinger, *The Ecclesiology of Vatican II*, 5.

Mary was not sent out to the world as the apostles were, but the personal journey outside of the self to the other, and so back to the self in mutual reciprocation (which is the life of the Trinity and of the missionary Church), is exemplified in the person of Mary. It is on the Cross, with Mary humbly attentive beneath it, that this pilgrimage finds its crux. The Mass, as the continuing and efficacious embodiment of the Cross, is the centre of the revelation of who the Church is and what her mission is.[4] Even with the sparseness of explicit focus on her actions in Scripture, it is not very difficult to see Mary's missionary drive as she, rising from that contemplative encounter with the Trinity mediated by the angel, swiftly runs to Elizabeth in witness to the great deeds of the Almighty. And there her identity as God's mother was proclaimed. After a long historical sundering of the cloister and ministry, saints Thomas Aquinas and Bonaventure unequivocally defended theirs and other congregation's somewhat revolutionary ethos as 'contemplative apostles'. Missionary monks, formed contemplatively in the cloister, taking same to the world, and returning for replenishment to the cloister, became models of the Christian life. So, liturgically, we come into the centre of the Mass which comes to us in Communion, go out as ministering missionaries and return to the Mass to be replenished.

In this light, Ratzinger warns against a 'dangerous new triumphalism, a tendency to which precisely the very critics of the old triumphalism often succumb'. The truth, as evident from our exploration of the Marian trajectory so far, is that 'so long as the Church is in pilgrimage on the earth, she has no ground to boast of her own works. Such self-glorification could become more dangerous than the *Sedia gestatoria* and the tiara, which are more likely to elicit a smile than a feeling of pride.'[5] Like Mary, whose 'yes' found its completion under the Cross, 'the place of the Church on earth can only be near the cross'.[6] The Marian compassionate passion under the Cross becomes a light for the Church and all her members in the call to reciprocal *kenosis*. It becomes a summons so 'that as we recall the sufferings

---

4   From another angle, though not unconnected with it, Jean Daniélou has written brilliantly on prayer as the Church's mission. J. Daniélou, *Prayer: The Mission of the Church* (Grand Rapids, MI: William B Eerdmans Publishing Co, 1996).

5   Ratzinger and Messori, *The Ratzinger Report*, 13.

6   Ibid.

shared by the Blessed Virgin Mary, we may with the Church fulfill in ourselves what is lacking in the sufferings of Christ'.[7] The Church as the Body of Christ necessarily implies taking the path trodden by her master. She is a living image of the self-sacrificial 'yes' of Christ, a prolongation of his *kenosis*.

Hence, Ratzinger's theology of election becomes crucial for the Church, both in her self-identification and mission. As earlier seen,[8] for Ratzinger, just as for Balthasar, election means being elected for another, for the sake of the non-elected. Indeed, as in Christ, the 'rejected one', it even implies being rejected. It is evidenced in the case of Israel, whose election as a particular people presaged and was the harbinger (already understood by some prophets) of the general proffer of salvation fulfilled in the universal Church. Thus, the Church's singularity like the light on the bushel is for the sake of others – her being is missionary. Parallel to this, individual election is for the potential salvation of others. Baptism and chrismation sanctify us but make us at the same time bearers of Christ to others.

The personal nature of the Church, which shines out in Mary, thus safeguards the understanding of the Church as being for others. Her nature is her mission, and vice versa. She is, in and with Christ, on a self-immolating mission towards the redemption of all creation. This already defines what the Church's missionary attitude and goal ought to be, an attitude quite incompatible with any trace of triumphalism or superiority. We could associate this with Avery Dulles' fifth model of the Church – the Church as Servant. He makes a useful reference to the Pastoral Letter of Cardinal Cushing on 'The Servant Church', in which the Cardinal argues that the Church's role is not only proclamation but also service 'in her ministry of reconciliation, of binding up wounds, of suffering service, of healing'. Like Mary, in whom she is personified, she is called to be 'the Church of the poor, the Church that moves through history as a humble servant'.[9] Cushing concludes that as 'the Lord was the "man for others", so must the Church

---

7   Pope Paul VI, *Marialis Cultus*, 11.
8   Cf. Chapter 2.
9   J. Ratzinger, *Theological Highlights of Vatican II* (New York: Paulist Press, 1966), 60. Cf. Roten, 'Mary, " 'Personal Concretization of the Church" ', 281.

be "the community for others" '.[10] In some sense, the personal dimension of the Church enables the Christian attributes predicated to individual Christians to be applied to the Church herself. Hence, Congar asks, 'is it the individual alone who must be the servant and not the master, who must forgive offences, bless his enemies and not curse them?'[11]

The self-sacrificing nature and mission of the church apply, not only on the horizontal level towards creation, but, indeed, first and foremost, on the vertical level. She responds to and is in fact an answer to someone. She is not only for another; she is from and belongs to another. For Ratzinger, once again, this has a markedly feminine element. In 'Why I am still in the Church', Ratzinger paints the image of the Church as the moon whose light is totally dependent on the light of the sun – on Jesus Christ, the eternal Sun of Justice. According to him, from primeval religious symbolism, the moon has been the 'symbol of fecundity as of weakness, of death and dissolution as of hope in rebirth [...] "at once pathetic and comforting" '. He underscores the fact that the Fathers of the Church found this moon-symbolism relevant for two reasons: the moon is associated with the woman (mother). 'Lunar symbolism becomes both a symbol for man and for humanity as represented by the woman, who is passive and fruitful from the power of what she receives.'[12] The imagery, here, is applicable to all of humanity, all of creation. As we earlier noted,[13] while presenting Mary as the feminine model, the figure of Mary is for all creation and not a model to 'subjugate the woman by exalting her'.

The second reason for evoking lunar symbolism is that, like the moon, the Church's light (power, holiness etc.), is only a 'borrowed light'. In herself, she 'is darkness, but sends out light from another'.[14] Just as space travellers have explored the moon 'merely as rock, desert, sand, mountains, and

---

10   R. Cushing, *The Servant Church* (Boston, MA: Daughters of St Paul, 1966), 7, 8; Cf. Dulles, *Models of the Church*, 92–93.

11   Y. Congar, *Power and Poverty in the Church* (Baltimore, MD: Helicon Press, 1964), 65; Cf. Dulles, *Models of the Church*, 101.

12   J. Ratzinger, 'Why I Am Still in the Church', in H. U. von Balthasar and J. Ratzinger (eds), *Two Say Why*, 77.

13   Cf. Chapter 7.

14   Cf. Ibid.; Roten, 'Mary, "Personal Concretization of the Church" ', 243.

so on, and never as light', so it is with the Church: 'If one travels round it and digs it up with the techniques of the space-traveler, one finds only deserts, sand, and rocks – the human qualities of man and his history, with its deserts, its dust and its heights. That is proper to it. Yet that is not the most characteristic thing about it. The decisive thing is that although it is intrinsically no more than sand and stone, it is also light from the Lord, from someone other than itself.'[15] This further accentuates the Church's nothingness and her sacramental nature. Counting for nothing in herself is actually her essence, for she 'exists only to be dispossessed', and it is in that dispossession that her essence lies. The only ground of her existence, the thing about her that counts, according to Ratzinger, happens to be that which she is not. *His* Church is the only thing that matters, not *ours* for 'a Church that is no more than *our* Church is a useless sandcastle.'[16]

Such a Marian dispossession is the key to missionary fruitfulness. As Ratzinger observes, 'more than ever before the Lord today has made us conscious of the fact that he alone can save his Church. The Church belongs to Christ and she depends on him to care for her. We are called upon to work with all our might, without anxiety and with the composure of one who knows that he is a useless servant even when he has done his full duty [...] patience, that daily form of love, is called for.'[17] The image of the patient and hopeful waiting of the holy soil becomes the true demeanour of a true and fruitful missionary Church: 'What we need, then, is to abandon this one-sided, Western activistic outlook, lest we degrade the Church to a product of our creation and design. The Church is not a manufactured item; she is, rather, the living seed of God that must be allowed to grow and ripen. This is why the Church needs the Marian mystery; this is why the Church herself is a Marian mystery. There can be fruitfulness in the Church only when she has this character, when she becomes holy soil for the Word. We must retrieve the symbol of the fruitful soil; we must once

15   J. Ratzinger, 'Why I Am Still in the Church', in H. U. von Balthasar and J. Ratzinger (eds), *Two Say Why*, 78.

16   Cf. Ibid., 78–80.

17   Ratzinger and Messori, *The Ratzinger Report*, 14.

more become waiting, inwardly recollected people who in the depth of
prayer, longing and faith give the Word room to grow.'[18]

   We are left with the difficulty of deciphering how the Church can at
the same time be the 'living seed of God' and 'fruitful soil for this seed'.
How can she, at the same time, be both active and passive? Perhaps in this
way. The seed is primarily the Word of God – Christ. But, in Ratzinger's
thought, Christianity is a call to become word in the Word. Similarly, the
soil in its very availability becomes seed in the Seed. This is another instance of that deeply Christian and Marian harmony between divine and
human instigation, activity and passivity. The seventeenth century poet
Richard Crashaw's marvellous phrase 'Love's Passives are his Activ'st Part'
is very apt here.

Ministry as Living the Marian Mystery

Ratzinger so dislikes any model of the church as an impersonal organization, for 'a Marian understanding of the Church is totally opposed to the
concept of the Church as a bureaucracy', an organization run by functionaries. The personal nature of the Church, necessarily consisting of a 'yes',
a surrendering (worshipful/holy) attitude, also defines ministering in the
Church. The Church's nature and mission of sacrificial service, total surrender, as the 'handmaid of the Lord', or what Louis-Marie de Montfort
has designated as 'slave',[19] not only obliges her to take the humble pos-
ture of self-effacing service but is the only guarantee of the credibility of
her authority. Her being nothing but grace is at one and the same time
both humbling and empowering. Ratzinger laments the 'decline of the

---

18   J. Ratzinger, 'My Word Shall Not Return to Me Empty', in H. U. von Balthasar and
     J. Ratzinger, *Mary: The Church*, 16–17.

19   In that concept of 'Holy Slavery', we find de Montfort's remedy to his critique,
     which is cited by Ratzinger, as we earlier saw: ' "You do much, but nothing comes of
     it" (Hg 1:6)!' J. Ratzinger, 'My Word Shall Not Return to Me Empty', in H. U. von
     Balthasar and J. Ratzinger, *Mary: The Church*, 16; Cf. Chapter 8.

authentic concept of "obedience"' in and to the Church: 'According to some it would no longer even be a Christian virtue but a heritage of an authoritarian, dogmatic past, hence one to be overcome.' This is the consequence of the wrong notion of Church as completely ours to make, plan and run at will: 'If the Church, in fact, is *our* Church, if *we alone* are the Church, if her structures are not willed by Christ, then it is no longer possible to conceive of the existence of a hierarchy as a service to the baptized established by the Lord himself.'[20]

Authentic ministry/authority in the Church and true mission entails being in Mary's position at the foot of Cross in humble service of the Body of Christ. It is this same stance that gives the authority for ministry, not only by Jesus' principle of the least as the greatest, but by the fact that owning nothing and owing everything to Christ legitimizes the authority of ministry as representative of Christ. It could be said, then, that the goal of ministry is wholly Christ. It is from and for Christ – head and members. Thus, ministry reflects the Church's innermost relational dynamics. The relational harmony of 'being from' and 'being for', is constitutive of Christian ministry. The power to serve is from self-surrender. Its nothingness is its strength. The Church's self-understanding as Marian mystery is the sure safeguard of this truth.

This, in turn, means that the binding force of ministerial service in the Church is not necessarily tied to the piety of the minister. Holiness (which could be described as the perfection of the 'yes' to God; tranquillity with the fact of being 'from' and 'for') is clearly the ideal habitat for the fruitful exercise of ministry, both on the part of the minister and the ministered to. Yet holiness is also the goal, the end, of ministry. If ministry were absolutely through and dependent on it, then it would not be truly 'from'. It would be, so to say, totally based on, and dependent on, the minister. Ratzinger, hence, insists that ministry has an independent legitimate authorization, such that, its rejection is the 'rejection of the concept of an authority willed by God, an authority therefore that has its legitimation in God and not – as happens in political structures – in the consensus of the majority of the members of an organization'.[21] For him, obedience to

20 Ratzinger, *The Ratzinger Report*, 49.
21 Ibid.

the legitimate ecclesiastical hierarchies is both necessary and fruitful. But this can only be realized within a vivid awareness, by the hierarchy and everyone else, of the truth that the Church and all she has are Christ's. It is not our invention, 'not a party, not an association, not a club'. This is because 'her deep and permanent structure is not *democratic* but *sacramental*, consequently *hierarchical*. For the hierarchy based on the apostolic succession is the indispensable condition to arrive at the strength, the reality of sacrament. Here authority is not based on the majority of votes; it is based on the authority of Christ himself, which he willed to pass on to men who were to be his representatives until his definitive return.'[22]

The nature and scope of authority has often been a cause of clashes in the Church. But, in Ratzinger's opinion, the root cause is essentially a 'God crisis'. Where the message of the centrality of God's action, as seen in the Virgin Motherhood of Mary (and, supposedly, in the liturgy as *actio divina*) is upheld, the time-honoured competition as to 'who is the greatest' is evaded. Much of the clamour for and against the reform of particular ministries in the Church will become irrelevant. One sees the wisdom of John Paul II's words, cited by Ratzinger, that 'the Church of today does not need any new reformers. The Church needs new saints.'[23] The humbling and empowering realization, on the part of the entire Church, that ministry is really 'from' and 'for' the Lord, mirrors once again the graceful Marian profile in the 'yes' (fiat). There is, thus, manifest wisdom in von Balthasar's submission in a pre-conciliar essay, "Who Is the Church?", which de Lubac synopsises thus: 'The Church is essentially bride. The masculine dimension of official ministry is subservient to the feminine dimension of active receptivity.'[24] Ministering in the Church, on all levels, becomes a call to be Marian, to become a 'yes'. Hence, Ratzinger insists: 'The Church, I shall never tire of repeating it, needs saints more than functionaries.'[25]

---

22   Ibid.
23   Ibid., 42–43.
24   A. Dulles, 'Mary Since Vatican II: Decline and Recovery', *Marian Studies* 53 (2002), 14. <http://ecommons.udayton.edu/marian_studies/vol53/iss1/5> (Accessed: 15 March 2021); Cf. H. U. von Balthasar, *Explorations in Theology II: Spouse of the Word* (San Francisco, CA: Ignatius Press, 1991), 157–166.
25   Ibid., 67.

The Unitive Mission

It was Ratzinger's hope that the insertion of the Marian treatise into the treatise on the Church would not only help to reveal the true image of the Church, but also that it 'may have brought us nearer to the time when it will again be conceivable that Christians of different denominations will understand one another on this particularly divisive issue'.[26] Such were the hopes of those in the Patristic School who vehemently fought for this inclusion. It is important, as Heim has argued, that besides the Protestant pressure from his native Germany, Patristic theology was a significant formative influence on Ratzinger's ecumenical consciousness. Heim quotes Stephen O. Horn who observes that 'Ratzinger is intent on countering a "denominationalism of division" with a "hermeneutic of unification"'.[27] Ratzinger's Mariology always has an oecumenical dimension. He is explicit about this: 'In the ecumenical sphere today one deplores that not enough was done in the past to prevent incipient divisions through a greater openness to reconciliation and to an understanding of the different groups. Well, that should apply as a behavioural maxim for us too in the present time. We must commit ourselves to reconciliation, so long and so far as it is possible, and we must utilize all the opportunities granted to us for this purpose.'[28] Citing John Henry Newman, Ratzinger notes that one of the major inhibitions to ecumenism is the fact that 'non-Catholics are accustomed to regard devotion to Mary as encroaching upon the position of Jesus'.[29]

This is where the reflection on the 'yes' becomes especially relevant, as it demonstrates the subordinate, yet intrinsic and 'complementary', role of Mary in the salvific action of the *Logos*. It is owing to the gradual recognition of this fact that 'nowadays Protestants are making some timid efforts to recapture the figure of Mary'.[30] Luther, himself, seemed to have been in no

---

26 Ratzinger, *Theological Highlights of Vatican II*, 60; Cf. Roten, 'Mary, "Personal Concretization of the Church"', 280.

27 Heim, *Joseph Ratzinger*, 516.

28 Ratzinger and Messori, *The Ratzinger Report*, 32.

29 J. Ratzinger, *God and the World: A Conversation with Peter Seewald* (San Francisco: Ignatius Press, 2002),.

30 Ibid., 302.

doubt regarding the privileged position of Mary: 'She is rightly called not only the Mother of the man, but also the Mother of God …. It is certain that Mary is the Mother of the real and true God.'[31] He believed that 'it is an article of faith that Mary is the Mother of the Lord and still a Virgin.'[32] There is, too, some convergence between Anglican and Catholic thinking in the agreed document of the 'Anglican – Roman Catholic International Commission (ARCIC)' which talks of a receiving together of the tradition of Mary's place in God's revelation.[33] It is significant how Anglicans and Catholics agree about the importance of Mary's consent. On this, the agreed statement reads:

> God's grace calls for and enables human response […] This is seen in the Gospel account of the Annunciation, where the angel's message evokes the response of Mary. The Incarnation and all that it entailed, including the passion, death and resurrection of Christ and the birth of the Church, came about by way of Mary's freely uttered fiat – 'let it be done to me according to your word' (Luke 1:38). We recognize in the event of the Incarnation God's gracious 'Yes' to humanity as a whole. This reminds us once more of the Apostle's words in 2 Corinthians 1:18–20 […] all God's promises find their 'Yes' in the Son of God, Jesus Christ. In this context, Mary's fiat can be seen as the supreme instance of a believer's 'Amen' in response to the 'Yes' of God. Christian disciples respond to the same 'Yes' with their own 'Amen'. They thus know themselves to be children together of the one heavenly Father, born of the Spirit as brothers and sisters of Jesus Christ, drawn into the communion of love of the blessed Trinity. Mary epitomizes such participation in the life of God. Her response was not made without profound questioning, and it issued in a life of joy intermingled with sorrow, taking her even to the foot of her son's cross. When Christians join in Mary's 'Amen' to the 'Yes' of God in Christ, they commit themselves to an obedient response to the Word of God, which leads to a life of prayer and service. Like Mary, they not only magnify the Lord with their lips: they commit themselves to serve God's justice with their lives. (cf. Luke 1:46–55)[34]

---

31   M. Luther cited in P. Haffner, *The Mystery of Mary* (Leominster: Gracewing, 2004), 6.

32   Ibid.

33   Anglican – Roman Catholic International Commission, *Mary: Grace and Hope in Christ*, 3, <http://www.prounione.urbe.it/dia-int/arcic/doc/e_arcic_mary02. html> (Version 4 July 2005, Accessed: 22 February 2021).

34   Ibid., 5.

One sees in this statement almost a recapitulation of the points we have made on the 'yes' of Mary. There appears a unanimous agreement on the meaning and role of the 'yes' and its implications for Mariology and for Christianity in general. Hence, the document concludes that 'it is impossible to be faithful to Scripture and not to take Mary seriously'.[35] From the 'The Evangelical [Protestant] Catechism for Adults' we read something quite similar and decisive: 'Mary is part of the gospel [...] She is presented as the one who listened in an exemplary way to the word of God, as the servant of the Lord saying yes to the word of God, as the full of grace who by herself is nothing, while she is everything by God's grace. Thus she is the original model of those who open themselves to God, and allow themselves to be enriched by him; she is the original model of the community of the believers, the Church. The receptive, motherly feminine element is not the worst part of the human reality, it is rather the best, and indeed the best of the Christian reality.'[36]

Besides this common inheritance and union in the 'yes' of Mary, Ratzinger also identifies auto-negation as the basis for brotherhood and this is the same self-emptying that characterizes Mary's 'yes'. Our 'yes' to the will of God, together in Mary, with Mary and in imitation of Mary, implies a brotherhood. Christian conversion and life, for Ratzinger, means 'to lose one's "oneself", to cease to regard one's own ego as an absolute'. It is a call to let the separating particularity of our own egos, the self-assertion of human selfhood, melt into the community of the new man Jesus Christ. It 'means losing one's own ego and becoming one in brotherhood with all those who are in Christ. As an ethic of true self-loss, it necessarily includes the brotherhood of all Christians'.[37] Thus, our union with Christ, which is effected in the 'yes', is also the basis for our union in Christ. The archetype of this is the Son of God's own taking on the form of a servant even to death on a cross, which is the occasion of his union with the Church. But precursor and exemplar in this is Mary under the cross who represents

---

35   Ibid., 6.

36   G. Bigotto, *Mary the Mother of Jesus: Exegesis and Spirituality* (Nairobi: Paulines Publications Africa, 2000), 77.

37   J. Ratzinger, *The Meaning of Christian Brotherhood* (San Francisco, CA: Ignatius Press, 1993), 54–55.

that church in her kenotic unity of being. This is the sense in Ratzinger's saying: 'Brotherhood is not seen naturalistically, as an original phenomenon of nature, but depends on a decision of the spirit, a saying "yes" to the will of God.'[38] That is why there is clear relation between Mary's being in affirmation to God and a true ecumenicism. The Incarnation of the Son of God is the fulfilment of God's will for the world. And, like Mary, our part in that fulfilment is the response of 'free and unqualified consent in utter self-giving and trust: "Behold I am the handmaid of the Lord; let it be done to me according to your word" (Lk 1:38; cf. Ps 123:2).'[39] This total self-donation in imitation of God himself, which is achieved and inaugurated for us in Mary, opens the way to brotherhood and communion. It thus becomes evident how 'God's kenosis is the place where the religions can meet without claims of sovereignty'.[40]

Ratzinger does not at all subscribe to the mistake of a 'praxeological priority', which upholds praxis rather than the standard of truth, as the hermeneutic of unity.[41] In condemning what he calls 'an unrestrained and unfiltered opening to the world', Ratzinger manifests his disapproval for an unguarded openness, which even 'brings up for discussion the very foundation of the *depositum fidei*'.[42] Proper ecumenism, for him, is not a matter of arbitrarily shifting grounds in compromise on the basic tenets of the deposit of the faith. Underneath the ensuing 'ecumenism of consensus' is a certain relativism that will mean the dissolution of ecumenism and even of the Church herself.[43] Hence, instead of an ecumenism of annexation, Ratzinger advocates for 'an onward "march … in faith under the leadership

---

38   Ibid., 26–27.

39   Anglican – Roman Catholic International Commission, *Mary*, 11.

40   J. Ratzinger, *Many Religions – One Covenant: Israel, the Church and the World* (San Francisco, CA: Ignatius Press, 1999), 108.

41   Cf. Heim, *Joseph Ratzinger*, 516. Sadly, in this clamour for consensus rather than unity, 'the belief that there is indeed truth, valid and binding truth, within history itself, in the figure of Jesus Christ and in the faith of the Church, is referred to as fundamentalism, which appears as the real assault upon the spirit of the modern age and, manifested in many forms, as the fundamental threat to the highest good of that age, freedom and tolerance'. J. Ratzinger, *Principles of Catholic Theology*, 120.

42   Ratzinger and V. Messori, *The Ratzinger Report*, 35.

43   Cf. Heim, *Joseph Ratzinger*, 516.

of the Lord" ', a march which will definitely mean a purification and renewal on all sides, a march in which statements are weighed 'in the context of the whole tradition and with a deeper understanding of Scripture'.[44] In this form of ecumenism, the splendour of Truth is allowed to shine, rather than disputing long-established customs. Tertullian reminded us that: 'Christ did not call himself the Custom, but rather the truth (*Virg.* I, I).'[45]

The Second Vatican Council 'proclaimed the duty of ecumenism as a search for true unity'.[46] Mary is a privileged gateway to that unity of truth, as we have repeatedly noted. (For instance, the understanding of the active surrender in grace in Mary, could be a key to the resolution of the original Catholic Protestant dispute over justification, which has been much clarified by the Joint Declaration – Catholics and Lutherans – of 1999.) A proper understanding of Mary's 'yes', as expounded by Ratzinger, is the harbinger of that unity which is at the heart of the Church's identity. For, as *Lumen Gentium* declares, the church is 'a sacrament ... a sign and instrument both of a very closely knit union with God and of the unity of the whole human race', leading all men to 'fuller unity in Christ'.[47]

44 Ibid., 517.
45 Cf. Ibid., 516–517.
46 Ratzinger, *The Ecclesiology of the Constitution on the Church*, 5.
47 LG I.

Bibliography

Primary Sources

Specific Sources

Mariological Works of J. Ratzinger

Ratzinger, J., *Daughter Zion: Meditations on the Church's Marian Belief*, Ignatius Press, San Francisco, CA, 1983 (Orig. *Die Tochter Zion: Betrachtungen über den Marienglauben der Kirche*, Johannes Verlag, Einsiedeln, 1977).

——, *Jesus of Nazareth: The Infancy Narratives*, Bloomsbury Publishing, London, 2012.

von Balthasar, H. U. and Ratzinger, J., *Mary: The Church at the Source*, Ignatius Press, San Francisco, CA, 2005 (Orig. *Kirche im Ursprung*, Verlag Herder, Freiburg im Breisgau 1980, 1981, 1985, Johannes Verlag, Einsiedeln, 1997, 2005).

Other Related Works of J. Ratzinger

Pope Benedict XVI, *Journey to Easter: Spiritual Reflections for the Lenten Season*, Crossroad Publishing Co., New York, 1987 (Orig. *Il cammino pasquale: Corso di Esercizi Spirituali tenuti in Vaticano alla presenza di S.S. Giovanni Paolo II.*, all'inizio della Quaresima 1983, Ancora, Milano, 1985, 1986, 2000, 2006).

Horn, S. O. and Pfnür, V. (eds), *God Is Near Us: The Eucharist, the Heart of Life*, Ignatius Press, San Francisco, CA, 2003 (Orig. *Gott ist uns nah. Eucharistie: Mitte des Lebens*, St Ulrich Verlag, Augsburg, 2001).

——, *Pilgrim Fellowship of Faith: The Church as Communion*, Ignatius Press, San Francisco, CA, 2005 (Orig. *Weggemeinschaft des Glaubens: Kirche als Communio*, St Ulrich Verlag, Augsburg, 2002, 2005).

Ratzinger, J., *Theological Highlights of Vatican II*, Paulist Press, New York, 1966 (Orig. *Die erste Sitzungsperiode des Zweiten Vatikanischen Konzils: Ein Rückblick*, Bachem, Köln, 1963).

——, *Dogma and Preaching*, Franciscan Herald Press, Chicago, 1985 (Orig. *Dogma und Verkündigung*, Erich Wewel Verlag, München, 1973).

——, *Behold the Pierced One: An Approach to a Spiritual Christology*, Ignatius Press, San Francisco, CA, 1986 (Orig. *Schauen auf den Durchbohrten: Versuche zu einer spirituellen Christologie*, Johannes Verlag, Einsiedeln, 1984, 1990).

——, *Feast of Faith: Approaches to a Theology of the Liturgy*, Ignatius Press, San Francisco, CA, 1986 (Orig. *Das Fest des Glaubens: Versuche zur Theologie des Gottesdienstes*, Johannes Verlag, Einsiedeln, 1981).

——, *Principles of Catholic Theology: Building Stones for a Fundamental Theology*, Ignatius Press, San Francisco, CA, 1987 (Orig. *Theologische Prinzipienlehre: Bausteine zur Fundamental theologie*, Erich Wewel Verlag, München, 1982).

——, *Church, Ecumenism and Politics*, St Paul's Publications, Slough, 1988 (Orig. *Kirche, Ökumene und Politik: Neue Versuche zur Ekklesiologie*, Johannes Verlag, Einsiedeln, 1987).

——, *Mary: God's Yes to Man*, Ignatius Press, San Francisco, CA, 1988 (Orig. *Das Zeichen der Frau: Versuch einer Hinführung zur Enzyklika «Redemptoris Mater» von Papst Johannes Paul II*, in Johannes Paul II, *Maria – Gottes Ja zum Menschen: Enzyklika 'Mutter des Erlösers' [Redemptoris Mater]*, Herder, Freiburg-Basel-Wien, 1987, 105–128).

——, 'Retrieving the Tradition: Concerning the Notion of Person in Theology', in *Communio* 17.3 (1990), 439–454 (Orig. Speck, J. (ed.), *Das Personverständnis in der Pädagogik und ihren Nachbarwissenschaften*, Verlag F. Kamp, Münster, 1966, 157–171).

——, *The Meaning of Christian Brotherhood*, Ignatius Press, San Francisco, CA, 1993 (Orig. *Die christliche Brüderlichkeit*, in *Der Seelsorger* 26 (1958), 387–429).

——, *'In the Beginning …' A Catholic Understanding of the Story of Creation and the Fall*, Wm. B. Eerdmans Publishing Co., Grand Rapids, MI, 1995 (Orig. *Im Anfang schuf Gott: Vier Münchener Fastenpredigten über Schöpfung und Fall – Konsequenzen des Schöpfungsglaubens*, Johannes Verlag, Einsiedeln, 1996/2005).

——, *The Nature and Mission of Theology: Approaches to Understanding Its Role in the Light of Present Controversy*, Ignatius Press, San Francisco, CA, 1995 (Orig. *Wesen und Auftrag der Theologie: Versuche zu ihrer Ortsbestimmung im Disput der Gegenwart*, Johannes Verlag, Einsiedeln, 1993).

——, *Called to Communion: Understanding the Church Today*, Ignatius Press, San Francisco, CA, 1996 (Orig. *Zur Gemeinschaft gerufen: Kirche heute verstehen*, Herder Verlag, Freiburg, 1991, 1992).

——, *A New Song for the Lord: Faith in Christ and Liturgy Today*, Crossroad Herder, New York, 1997 (Orig. *Ein neues Lied für den Herrn: Christusglaube und Liturgie in der Gegenwart*, Verlag Herder, Freiburg im Breisgau, 1995).

——, 'The Holy Spirit as Communio: Concerning the Relationship of Pneumatology and Spirituality in Augustine', in *Communio* 25.2 (1998), 324–339 (Orig. *Der Heilige Geist als communio: Zum Verhältnis von Pneumatologie und Spiritualität bei Augustinus*, in Heitmann, V. C. and Mühlen, H. (eds), *Erfahrung und Theologie des Heiligen Geistes*, Hamburg-München, 1974, 223–238).

——, *Milestones: Memoirs, 1927–1977*, Ignatius Press, San Francisco, CA, 1998 (Orig. *Aus meinem Leben: Erinnerungen* (1927–1977), Deutsche Verlags – Anstalt, Stuttgart, München, 1998).

——, *Many Religions, One Covenant: Israel, the Church and the World*, Ignatius Press, San Francisco, CA, 1999 (Orig. *Die Vielfalt der Religionen und der Eine Bund*, Verlag Urfeld, Hagen, 1998).

——, *The Spirit of the Liturgy*, Ignatius Press, San Francisco, CA, 2000 (Orig. *Der Geist der Liturgie*, Herder, Freiburg im Breisgau, 2000).

——, 'The Ecclesiology of the Constitution on the Church, Vatican II, "Lumen Gentium"', in *L'Osservatore Romano*, English Edition, Baltimore, MD, 19 September 2001, 5 (Orig. *Deutsche Tagespost*, Sonderbeilage (März 2000), 1–8).

——, 'The Feeling of Things, the Contemplation of Beauty', in *L'Osservatore Romano*, English Edition, Baltimore, 45 (6 November 2002), 6–7 (Orig. *Il sentimento delle cose, la contemplazione della Bellezza/Der Sinn für die Dinge, die Betrachtung des Schönen* [Messaggio al XXIII Meeting (Comunione e Liberazione) per l'amicizia fra i popoli, Rimini, 21 agosto 2002], *30 Tage 20* (2002), 9, 60–65; Litterae communionis – Spuren (September 2002), 24–28).

——, *Introduction to Christianity*, Ignatius Press, San Francisco, CA, 2004 (Orig. *Einführung in das Christentum: Vorlesungen über das Apostolische Glaubensbekenntis*, Kösel Verlag, München, 1968).

——, *Truth and Tolerance: Christian Belief and World Religions*, Ignatius Press, San Francisco, CA, 2004 (Orig. *Glaube – Wahrheit – Toleranz: Das Christentum und die Weltreligionen*, Verlag Herder, Freiburg im Breisgau, 2003).

——, *On the Way to Jesus Christ*, Ignatius Press, San Francisco, CA, 2005 (Orig. *Unterwegs zu Jesus Christus*, Sankt-Ulrich-Verlag, Augsburg, 2003).

——, *Values in a Time of Upheaval*, Ignatius Press, San Francisco, CA, 2006 (Orig. *Werte in Zeiten des Umbruchs: Die Herausforderungen der Zukunft bestehen*, Herder Verlag, Freiburg, 2005/Libreria Editrice Vaticana, Città del Vaticano, 2005).

——, *Jesus of Nazareth*, I, Doubleday, New York, 2007.

——, *Jesus of Nazareth*, II, Ignatius Press, San Francisco, CA, 2011.

Ratzinger, J. and Messori, V., *The Ratzinger Report: An Exclusive Interview on the State of the Church*, Ignatius Press, San Francisco, CA, 1985 (Orig. *Zur Lage des Glaubens: Ein Gespräch mit Vittorio Messori*, Verlag Neue Stadt, München, Zürich, Wien, 1985, 2006).

Ratzinger, J. and Pera, M., *Without Roots: The West, Relativism, Christianity, Islam*, Books Group, New York, 2006 (Orig. *Senza radici: Europa, Relativismo, Cristianesimo, Islam*, Mondadori, Milano, 2004, 2005).

Ratzinger, J. and Seewald, P., *God and the World: A Conversation with Peter Seewald*, Ignatius Press, San Francisco, CA, 2000 (Orig. *Gott und die Welt: Glauben und Leben in unserer Zeit, Ein Gespräch mit Peter Seewald*, Deutsche Verlags-Anstalt Stuttgart, München, 2000, 2001).

——, *Salt of the Earth: Christianity and the Catholic Church at the End of the Millennium*, Ignatius Press, San Francisco, CA, 1997 (Orig. *Salz der Erde: Christentum und katholische Kirche an der Jahrtausendwende, Ein Gespräch mit Peter Seewald*, Deutsche Verlags-Anstalt Stuttgart, München, 1996, 1997).

Schindler, D. L. (ed.), *Joseph Ratzinger in Communio*, William B. Eerdmans Publishing Company, Grand Rapids, MI, 2010 (Orig. *Werte in Zeiten des Umbruchs*, Verlag Herder, Freiburg im Breisgau, 2005).

von Balthasar, H. U. and Ratzinger, J. (eds), *Two Say Why*, Search Press Ltd and Franciscan Herald Press, London and Chicago, 1971 (Orig. *Zwei Plädoyers: Warum ich noch ein Christ bin – Warum ich noch in der Kirche bin*, Abendvorträge am 4 und 11 Juni 1970 in München auf Einladung der Katholischen Akademie in Bayern Kösel, 1971, Münchener Akademie-Schriften, 57).

Works on J. Ratzinger

Bardazzi, M., *Nella Vigna del Signore: La Vita di Joseph Ratzinger, Papa Benedetto XVI*, RCS Libri, Milano, 2005.

Boeve, L. and Mannion, G. (eds), *The Ratzinger Reader: Mapping a Theological Journey*, T&T Clark International, New York, 2010.

Cavadini, J. C. (ed.), *Explorations in the Theology of Benedict XVI*, University of Notre Dame Press, Notre Dame, 2016.

Dulles, A., 'From Ratzinger to Benedict', *First Things* (February 2006), New York, 2006, 24–29.

Gaál, E. de, *O Lord, I Seek Your Countenance. Explorations and Discoveries in Pope Benedict XVI's Theology*, Emmaus Academic, Steubenville, 2018.

Heim, M. H., *Joseph Ratzinger: Life in the Church and Living Theology: Fundamentals of Ecclesiology*, Ignatius Press, San Francisco, CA, 2007.

Mansfield, S., *Pope Benedict XVI: His Life and Mission*, Penguin Group, New York, 2005.

Masciarelli, M. G., *Il Segno della Donna: Maria nella teologia di Joseph Ratzinger*, edizione San Paolo, Milano, 2007.

McKenna, F. M., *Innovation within Tradition: Joseph Ratzinger and Reading the Women of Scripture*, Fortress Press, Minneapolis, MN, 2015.

Moynihan, R. (ed.), *Let God's Light Shine Forth: The Spiritual Vision of Pope Benedict XVI*, Doubleday, New York, 2005.

Nichols, A., *The Thought of Benedict XVI: An Introduction to the Theology of Joseph Ratzinger*, Burns & Oates, London, 2005.

Perry, T., *The Theology of Benedict XVI. A Protestant Appreciation*, Lexham Press, Bellingham, 2019.

Roten, J. G., 'Mary, "Personal Concretization of the Church": Elements of Benedict XVI's Marian Thinking', in *Marian Studies* 57 (2006), 243–321.

Rowland, T., *Ratzinger's Faith: The Theology of Pope Benedict XVI*, Oxford University Press, New York, 2008.

Staglianò, A., *Madre di Dio. La mariologia personalistica di Joseph Ratzinger*, Edizioni San Paolo, Milano, 2010.

Thornton, J. F. and Varenne, S. B. (eds), *The Essential Pope Benedict XVI: His Central Writings and Speeches*, Harper Collins Publishers, New York, 2007.

Tilley, R. H., *Benedict XVI and the Search for Truth*, Gracewing, Leominster, 2008.

Tosatti, M., *Il dizionario di papa Ratzinger: Guida al Pontificato*, Baldini Castoldi Dalai, Milano, 2005.

Twomey, D. V., *Pope Benedict XVI, The Conscience of Our Age: A Theological Portrait*, Ignatius Press, San Francisco, CA, 2007.

Wojtczak, A., 'The Characteristic Aspects of Benedict XVI's Teaching on Mary', in *Gregorianum* 95. 2 (2014), 327–348.

General Sources

Sacred Scriptures

The Holy Bible, Revised Standard Version, Catholic Truth Society, London, 1966.

The New Jerusalem Bible, Standard Edition, Doubleday Dell Publishing Group, Inc., New York, 1985.

Magisterium

Church Documents
Catechism of the Catholic Church, Libreria Editrice Vaticana, Roma, 1994.

Flannery, A. (ed.), *Vatican Council II: The Conciliar and Post Conciliar Documents*, Dominican Publications, Dublin, 1975, 1987.

Second Vatican Council, *Sacrosanctum Concilium*, The Constitution on the Sacred Liturgy, 4 December 1963: AAS 56 (1964), 97–144; EV I, 1–244.

——, *Lumen Gentium*, Dogmatic Constitution on the Church, 21 November 1964: AAS 57 (1965), 5–75; EV I, 284–456.

——, *Ad Gentes*, Decree on the Mission Activity of the Church, 7 December 1965: AAS 58 (1966), 947–990; EV I, 1087–1242.

——, *Dei Verbum*, Dogmatic Constitution on Divine Revelation, 18 November 1965: AAS 58 (1966), 817–835; EV I, 1087–1242.

——, *Gaudium et Spes*, Pastoral Constitution on the Church in the Modern World, 7 December 1965: AAS 58 (1966), 1025–1120; EV I, 1319–1644.

Vorgrimler, H. et al. (eds), *Commentary on the Documents of Vatican II*, vol. 1, Herder and Herder, New York, 1967.

Papal Documents and Other Pontifical Writings
Benedict XVI, Pope, *Homily for the Beginning of the Petrine Ministry of the Bishop of Rome* (Vatican 2005), AAS 97 (2005), 710.

——, *Verbum Domini, Post-Synodal Apostolic Exhortation to the Bishops, Clergy, Consecrated Persons and the Lay Faithful on the Word of God in the Life and Mission of the Church* (Vatican 2010), EV 26, 2218–2433.

Calkins, A. B. (a cura di), *Totus Tuus: Il Magistero Mariano di Giovanni Paolo II*, Edizioni Cantagalli, Siena, 2006.

John Paul II, Pope, 'Apostolic Letter for the 1600th Anniversary of the First Council of Constantinople and the 1550th Anniversary of the Council of Ephesus' (Vatican 1981), in *IGPII*, IV, 1 (1981), 815–828.

——, *Redemptoris Mater, Encyclical on the Blessed Virgin Mary in the Life of the Pilgrim Church* (Vatican 1987), EV 10, 1272–1421.

——, 'Letter to All Consecrated Persons Belonging to Religious Communities and Secular Institutes on the Occasion of the Marian Year' (Vatican 1988), in *IGPII*, XI, 2 (1988), 1590–1602.

——, 'Letter to Priests for Holy Thursday' (Vatican 1988), in *IGPII*, XI, 1 (1988), 721–733.

——, *Mulieris Dignitatem, Apostolic Letter on the Dignity and Vocation of Women, on the Occasion of the Marian Year* (Vatican 1988), EV 11, 1206–1345.

——, *Tertio Millennio Adveniente, Apostolic Letter to the Bishops, Clergy and Lay Faithful on Preparation for the Jubilee of the Year 2000* (Vatican 1994), EV 14, 1714–1820.

——, *Evangelium Vitae, Encyclical Letter to the Bishops Priests and Deacons Men and Women Religious Lay Faithful and all People of Good Will on the Value and Inviolability of Human Life* (Vatican 1995), EV 14, 1588–1716.

——, *Rosarium Virginis Mariae, Apostolic Letter to the Bishops, Clergy and Faithful on the Most Holy Rosary* (Vatican 2002), EV 21, 1167–1250.

——, *Ecclesia de Eucharistia, Encyclical Letter to the Bishops, Priests and Deacons, Men and Women in the Consecrated Life and All the Lay Faithful on the Eucharist in Its Relationship to the Church* (Vatican 2003), EV 24, 213–325.

——, *Memory & Identity: Personal Reflections*, Orion Books Ltd, London, 2005.

Leo XIII, Pope, *Octobri Mense, Encyclical on the Rosary* (Vatican 1891), AAS 24 (1891–1892), 193–203.

Paul VI, Pope, *Signum Magnum, Apostolic Exhortation on Venerating and Imitating the Virgin Mary, Mother of the Church and Model of All Virtues* (Vatican 1967), EV 2, 1177–1193.

——, *Marialis Cultus, Apostolic Exhortation for the Right Ordering and Development of Devotion to the Blessed Virgin Mary* (Vatican 1974), EV 7, 13–97.

——, *Gaudete in Domino, Apostolic Exhortation on Christian Joy* (Vatican 1975), EV 5, 1243–1313.

——, 'Letter to Cardinal Léon Jozef Suenens on the Occasion of the International Marian Congress, (Vatican 1975)', in *IPVI*, XIII (1976), 495–496.

Pius IX, Pope, 'Ineffabilis Deus, Apostolic Constitution on the Immaculate Conception' (Vatican 1854), in DS 2803.

Pius XII, Pope, *Munificentissimus Deus, Apostolic Constitution on Assumption* (Vatican 1975), AAS 42 (1950), 753–771.

Other Ecclesiastical Documents

Anglican – Roman Catholic International Commission, *Mary: Grace and Hope in Christ*, Morehouse Publishing, London, 2005.

Congregation for Catholic Education, *The Virgin Mary in Intellectual and Spiritual Formation*, Rome, 25 March 1988, EV 11, 283–324.

Congregation for the Doctrine of the Faith, *Some Aspects of the Church Understood as Communion*, Letter to the Bishops of the Catholic Church, 28 June 1992.

The Divine Office, *Liturgy of the Hours, According to the Roman Rite*, The Talbot Press Ltd, Dublin, 1974.

National Conference of Catholic Bishops, *Behold Your Mother: Woman of Faith – A Pastoral Letter on the Blessed Virgin Mary*, 21 November 1973,

Publications Office, Washington, DC, United States Catholic Conference, Washington, 1973.

Sacred Congregation for the Clergy, *General Catechetical Directory*, 18 March 1971.

Church Fathers and Classics

Gregory of Palamas, 'A Homily on the Dormition of Our Supremely Pure Lady Theotokos and Ever-Virgin Mary' (Homily 37), in PG 151, 472.

Newman, J. H., *An Essay on the Development of Christian Doctrine*, University of Notre Dame Press, Notre Dame, IN, 1989.

Roberts, A. and Donaldson, J. (eds), *The Ante-Nicene Fathers*, rev. ed., vols I, III, VI, T&T Clark, Edinburgh, 1993, 1996.

Scheeben, M. J., *Mariology*, B. Herder Book Co., London, 1946.

Thomas Aquinas, *Summa Theologica*, Christian Classics, Westminster, MD, 1948.

Secondary Sources

Studies on Mariology

Bearsley, J. P., 'Mary the Perfect Disciple: A Paradigm for Mariology', in *Theological Studies* 41.3 (1980), 461–504.

Bigotto, G., *Mary the Mother of Jesus: Exegesis and Spirituality*, Paulines Publications Africa, Nairobi, 2000.

Boss, S. J. (ed.), *Mary: The Complete Resource*, Continuum, London, 2007.

Brown, R. E., et al. (eds), *Mary in the New Testament*, Fortress Press, Philadelphia, PA, 1978.

Buby, B., *Mary of Galilee Vol. III: The Marian Heritage of the Early Church*, Society of St Paul, New York, 1997.

Carroll, E. R., *Understanding the Mother of Jesus*, Veritas Publications, Dublin, 1979.

Coletti, D., '*Vi fu uno sposalizio a Cana di Galilea': Lectio divina su Gv* 2.1–12, in: <https://www.chiesadimilano.it/wp-content/uploads/2017/04/Coletti_ _1.42703.pdf> (Accessed: 22 February 2021).

de Fiores, S., *Maria Madre di Gesu: Sintesistorico-salvifica*, EBD, Bologna, 2002.

Deiss, L., *Mary: Daughter of Zion*, The Liturgical Press, Collegeville, MN, 1972.

de La Potterie, I., *La Madre di Gesù e il mistero di Cana*, 'La Civiltà Cattolica', 130.4 (1979), 425–440.

——, *Mary in the Mystery of the Covenant*, Alba House, New York, 1992.

Friethoff, C. X. J. M., *A Complete Mariology*, The Newman Press, Westminster, MD, 1958.

Galligan, J. S., 'Mary: A Mosaic of Joy', *Review for Religious* 43 (January/February 1984), 82–92.

Haffner, P., *The Mystery of Mary*, Gracewing, Leominster, 2004.

Jelly, F. M., *Madonna: Mary in the Catholic Tradition*, Our Sunday Visitor Publishing Division, Indiana, 1986.

Kulandaisamy, D. S., 'The First "Sign" of Jesus at the Wedding at Cana. An Exegetical Study on the Function and Meaning of John 2.1–12', *Marianum* 68 (2006), 17–116.

Laurentin, R. et al. (eds), *Mary in Faith and Life in the New Age of the Church*, Franciscan Mission Press, Ndola, 1983.

Levering, M., *Mary's Bodily Assumption*, University of Notre Dame Press, Notre Dame, IN, 2014.

Liguori, A., *The Glories of Mary*, J. P. Kenedy & Sons, New York, 1888.

Livius, T., *The Blessed Virgin in the Fathers of the First Sixth Centuries*, Burns and Oates, London, 1893.

Manelli, S. M., *All Generations Shall Call Me Blessed: Biblical Mariology*, Academy of the Immaculate, Stockbridge, MA, 1995.

Manteau-Bonamy, H. M., *Immaculate Conception and the Holy Spirit: The Marian Teachings of Father Kolbe*, Franciscan Marytown Press, Kenosha, WI, 1977.

McBride, T. M., *The Marian Theology of Von Balthasar and the Proposed Definition of Mary Co-redemptrix*, <http://www.christendom-awake.org/pages /marian/ 5thdogma/mcbride.htm> (Version 19 April 2002, Accessed: 21 February 2021).

O'Carroll, M. (ed.), *Theotokos: A Theological Encyclopedia of the Blessed Virgin Mary*, Michael Glazier Inc., Wilmington, DE, 1982.

O'Carroll, M., *This Age and Mary*, The Mercier Press Limited, Dublin, 1946.

Papali, C., *Mother of God: Mary in Scripture and Tradition*, Augustine Publ. Co., Devon, 1987.

Rahner, K., *Mary, Mother of the Lord*, The Catholic Book Club, London, 1963.

Schillebeeckx, E., *Mary, Mother of the Redemption: The Religious Bases of the Mystery of Mary*, Shield and Ward, London, 1964.

Semmelroth, O., *Mary Archetype of the Church*, M. H. Gill and Son Limited, Dublin, 1963.

Serra, A., *Maria a Cana e presso la croce*, Madre della Chiesa, Roma, 1991.

——, *Nato da donna … (Gal 4,4): Ricerche bibliche su Maria di Nazaret (1989–1992)*, CENS-Marianum, Roma, 1992.

Shenuoda III, Patriarch, *The Holy Virgin St. Mary*, Transl. from the Arabic edition of 1999, in <https://st-takla.org/Feastes-&-Special-Events/Virgin-Mary-Fast/Saint-Mary-Fast_Virgin-Life-Hymns-mp3s-02-Pope-Shenouda-Virgin-Mary-Book.html>, (Accessed: 22 February 2021).

Suenens, L., *Mary the Mother of God*, Hawthorn Books, Inc., New York, 1959.

Other Studies

Barth, K., *Church Dogmatics III.I: The Doctrine of Creation*, Continuum International Publishing Group, New York, 2004.

Boselli, G. (ed.), *L'altare: mistero di presenza, opera dell'arte*, edizioni Qiqajon, Magnano, 2005.

Bouyer, L., *The Eternal Son: A Theology of the Word of God and Christology*, Our Sunday Visitor, Huntington, IN, 1978.

Burns, P. J. (ed.), *Mission and Witness: The Life of the Church*, Geoffrey Chapman, London, 1965.

Calabrese, G., Goyret, P., and Piazza O. F. (eds), *Dizionario di Ecclesiologia*, Città Nuova, Roma, 2010.

Congar, Y., *Power and Poverty in the Church*, Helicon, Baltimore, MD, 1964.

Cushing, R., *The Servant Church*, Daughters of St Paul, Boston, 1966.

Daniélou, J., *Prayer: The Mission of the Church*, William B Eerdmans Publishing Co, Grand Rapids, MI, 1996.

Drury, E. Y. J., *Tradition and Design in Luke's Gospel: A Study in Early Christian Historiography*, John Knox, Atlanta, GA, 1977.

Dulles, A., *Models of the Church*, Doubleday, New York, 1974.

Evdokimov, P., *The Art of the Icon: A Theology of Beauty*, Oakwood Publications, Torrance, CA, 1990.

Gallizzi, M., *La scelta dei poveri, Vangelo secondo Luca*, vol. I, Turin, 1985.

Guardini, R., *La Chiesa del Signore*, Morcelliana, Brescia, 1967.

——, *The Spirit of the Liturgy*, Morcelliana, Brescia, 1980.

Guthrie, D., 'John', in Carson, D. A. et al. (eds), *New Bible Commentary*, Inter-Varsity Press, Leicester, 1994, 1021–1065.

Hahn, S. (ed.), *Letter & Spirit, The Authority of Mystery: The Word of God and the People of God*, St Paul Center for Biblical Theology, Steubenville, OH, 2006.

Harrington, W. J., *Record of Fulfilment, The New Testament*, The Prior Press, Chicago, 1965.

Hugh, P., 'Holiness', in Herbermann, C. G. et al. (eds), *The Catholic Encyclopedia*, vol. 7, Robert Appleton Company, New York, 1910, 386–387.

Imoda, F., *A Journey to Freedom: An Interdisciplinary Approach to the Anthropology of Formation*, Peeters Publishers, Leuven, 2000.

Jurgens, J. B., *The Faith of the Early Fathers: Clement, Ignatius and Polycarp*, vol. 1, Baker Book House, Grand Rapids, MI, 1981.

Kasper, W., *The God of Jesus Christ*, The Crossroad Publishing Company, New York, 1992.

Kelly, A. J., 'Logos', in Komonchak, J. A. et al. (eds), *The New Dictionary of Theology*, Theological Publications in India, Bangalore, 1996, 601–602.

Komonchak, J. A. et al. (eds), *The New Dictionary of Theology*, Theological Publications in India, Bangalore, 1996.

Laurentin, R., *Truth of Christmas: Beyond the Myths*, St Bede's Publications, Petersham, 1986.

Marron, H. M., *Time and Timeliness*, Sheed and Ward, New York, 1969.

Molinski, W., 'Virginity', in Rahner, K. et al. (eds), *Sacramentum Mundi: An Encyclopedia of Theology*, vol. 6, Herder and Herder, New York, 1969, 333–336.

Nichols, A., *Holy Order: The Apostolic Ministry from the New Testament to the Second Vatican Council*, Veritas, Dublin, 1990.

——, *The Shape of Catholic Theology: An Introduction to Its Sources, Principles and History*, The Order of St Benedict, Inc., Collegeville, MN, 1991.

——, *Catholic Thought since the Enlightenment: A Survey*, Unisa Press, Pretoria, 1998.

——, *Redeeming Beauty: Soundings in Sacral Aesthetics*, Ashgate Publishing Limited, Hampshire, 2007.

Orlando, L., *Il Vangelo di Giovanni: Lettura Teologica*, Puntopace, Taranto, 2003.

Quasten, J., *Patrology*, vol. II, Christian Classics, Westminster, MD, 1986.

Saward, J., *Cradle of Redeeming Love: The Theology of the Christmas Mystery*, Ignatius Press, San Francisco, CA, 2002.

Schmaus, M., 'Mariology', in Rahner, K. et al. (eds), *Sacramentum Mundi: An Encyclopedia of Theology*, vol. 3, Herder and Herder, New York, 1969, 376–390.

Verheul, A., *Introduction to the Liturgy*, Anthony Clarke, Wheathampstead, 1972.

von Balthasar, H. U., *The Threefold Garland*, Ignatius Press, San Francisco, CA, 1982.

——, *The Office of Peter and the Structure of the Church*, Ignatius Press, San Francisco, CA, 1986.

——, *Theo-Drama*, vol. 3: *Dramatis Personae: Persons in Christ*, Ignatius Press, San Francisco, CA, 1992.

von Balthasar, H. U. et al., *Explorations in Theology II: Spouse of the Word*, Ignatius Press, San Francisco, CA, 1991.

Zevini, G., *Vangelo Secondo Giovanni*, vol. I, Città Nuova, Roma, 1984.

Zizioulas, J. D., *Being as Communion: Studies in Personhood and the Church*, Darton, Longman and Todd, London, 1985.

Index

Abraham's sacrifice 76
Actio Divina xvii, xxiii, xxiv, 66, 73, 75,
    77, 86, 98
actio of God 76
Adam-Christ 49
Allness 42, 71
Alpha and Omega xix, 39
altar 71–72, 75, 83–86, 88–89, 91
anachronistic 27
annexation 102
Annunciation 41, 49, 60–61, 64–65, 70,
    72, 81, 85, 100
anthropology 47, 115
anti-Christ 24
apostles xxvi
arbitrariness 28
Ark of the Covenant 50, 79
assumption 15–16, 111, 113
atheism 25
authoritarian 23, 97

baptism 17, 33, 83, 93
Barth, K. 114
beauty 57, 74, 107, 114, 115
Being as Communion 115
Benedictine Rule 40, 68
Bible xxvii, 48–49, 110, 115
Biblical Mariology 113
Bigotto, G. 112
bishop xxvi, 23, 25, 110
body of Christ 33, 41, 59, 81–83
Bouyer, L. 114
Bride of Christ 16, 35, 53, 61
brotherhood 101–102

Cardinal Julius Döpfner 7
Catechism of the Catholic Church 110
Catholic Church xxvii, 4, 10, 23, 27, 31, 38
Catholic theology 3–5, 14, 16, 40, 102,
    106, 115
Christ's body xxi, 36, 83
Christianity 19, 25, 40, 56, 65, 73, 79, 85,
    96, 101
Christocentric 14
Christological 34, 82
Christological mystery 35
Christology 16, 35, 59, 88, 106
Christomonism 35
Church xvii, xviii, xix, xxi, xxii, xxiii,
    xxiv, xxv, xxvii, 3–10, 13–18, 20,
    22–42, 45–61, 63–65, 68–73, 75,
    77–81, 83–86, 90–103, 105–116
Church Documents 110
Church Fathers 55
Church Fathers and Classics 112
Collegiality 40
Communion xviii, 21, 25, 31, 38, 41, 59, 60,
    65, 92, 100, 102, 105–107, 111, 115
Conciliar 29, 46, 69, 110
Congregation for Catholic Education 111
Congregation for the Doctrine of the
    Faith xxvii, 38, 111
conscience 109
consensus 23–24, 97, 102
conversion 4, 101
Council Fathers 24–26, 39, 77, 85
Council of Trent 27
Councils 27
Covenant 37, 48, 50, 67, 79, 83, 102, 107, 113

creation xxiii, 21, 37–38, 61, 64–65, 68, 75–76, 79, 93–95, 106, 114
Creed 35
Cross 21, 36–37, 60, 71, 83, 86, 89–90, 92, 97
crystallization 55
cultural revolution 5

Daniélou 114
Daughter Zion xxi, xxiii, xxv, 28, 33–34, 45, 47, 49–50, 52–53, 55, 58, 61, 63–64, 69, 71, 78, 82, 84
de Fiores, S. 112
Dei Verbum xxvii, 68, 110
Deiss, L. 112
demystification 38
depositum fidei 102
Divine Logos 21
divine maternity 53
divine volition 76
divinization 55, 77
Doctrine xxvii, 33, 35, 38, 45, 48, 52–55, 112, 114
dogma 106
dogmatic theology 23
Dulles, A. 108, 114

Ecclesia immaculata 49
Ecclesial 16, 91
ecclesiocentric Mariology 46
Ecclesiocentric Trajectory 14
ecclesiocentric typology 15
ecclesiological relativism 20
ecclesiology xvii, xviii, xix, 7–8, 13, 15–16, 20, 24, 28, 30–38, 40–41, 45–50, 52, 55–57, 59, 64, 69, 72–73
ecclesiology of communion 41
ecclesiotypical Mariology 47
ecumenical 31, 87, 99
ecumenism xxiii, 28, 36, 60, 99, 102, 103, 106
encyclical 34, 53, 110, 111

Enlightenment 20–21, 115
eschatological 22, 31, 41–42, 74, 83
eschatologically 37, 88
Eucharist xix, 33, 36–37, 39, 41, 61, 63, 67, 71, 73, 82–83, 89
Eucharistic assembly 33, 38
Eucharistic ecclesiology 24, 25, 30, 35, 37, 38, 41, 57
exaggerated humility 4, 5
Exegesis 101, 112
exegetical 60, 88, 113

faith 3, 6–7, 16, 21, 27–28, 37, 42, 51, 54, 58, 70, 80, 84, 86, 88–90, 96, 100, 102
Fall 106
family of God 17
Fathers of the Church 9, 19–20, 36, 60–61, 69, 94
Feast of Life 60
femininity 52
feminism 32
Freedom 40, 115
fruitfulness xviii, 17, 52–53, 80, 91, 95
fundamentalism 102

gate of heaven 88
Gate of the East 87–88
Gaudium et Spes xxvii, 6, 77, 110
Gnostic teaching 4
God xix, xxi, xxii, xxiii, xxiv, xxv, 17, 19–22, 25, 29–34, 36–39, 41–42, 47, 49–51, 53–61, 63–66, 68–71, 73–83, 85–92, 95–101, 103, 105–106, 108–110, 113–115
Godhead 47, 53
gospel 3, 5, 101
grace xix, xxiii, 16, 35, 42, 49, 53, 59, 66, 77, 81, 96, 100–101, 103

heaven 37, 54, 82–83, 90
hedonistic stamp 5

Hellenistic antecedent 40
hermeneutic xxii, 20, 34, 47, 66, 74,
 99, 102
holiness xxiv, 28, 42, 51, 94, 97
holiness 42, 97
Holy Remnant 50
Holy Soil' 50
Holy Spirit 17, 21, 30, 39, 47, 78–79, 107, 113
humility 34, 73

Idealism 20
Immaculate Conception 16, 48, 50, 61,
 81, 111, 113
immolation 37, 71, 90
Incarnate Word xix, 21, 38, 84
incarnation 21, 31, 49, 82
infallibility 23
intrinsic holiness 4
Iscariotan 76

Jelly, F.M. 113
Jesus 18, 38, 46, 60, 67, 70, 73, 76, 80, 81,
 90, 99, 105, 107–108, 112–113, 115
Jesus Christ 3, 17, 41, 49, 64, 78, 82, 86,
 94, 100–102
Joint Declaration 103

Kasper, W. 115
kenosis 37, 71, 92, 102

lethargy 5
liberal theology 23
liberalism 23
liberation theology 31
liturgy xxvii, 23, 50, 60, 63–67, 69, 71–
 74, 77, 82–83, 86–87, 89
Logos xix, xxiii, 21, 38, 40–41, 49, 51, 53,
 63, 74, 80–82, 84, 87, 89, 99, 115
Lord xviii, xxii, 6–7, 27, 33, 37, 39, 42, 53,
 55, 58, 60, 65, 70–71, 75, 78–80,
 82–84, 86, 88–91, 93, 95–96, 98,
 100–103

love 4, 21, 52, 55, 56, 61, 66, 80, 95, 100
Lumen Gentium xxiv, xxvii, 8, 15–18, 24,
 30, 39, 42, 46, 50, 59, 67, 78, 103,
 107, 110
Lutheran theologian 22

Magisterium 110
Magnificat 66, 70
man 65–66, 77, 89, 106
Marialis Cultus xxii, 16–17, 46, 61, 70,
 78, 86, 90
Marian ecclesiology 15, 40, 69, 73
Marian mystery xvii, xviii, xix, 57, 71,
 83, 95, 97
Marian treatise 45, 99
Mariologist 9
Mariology xvii, xviii, xix, xxi, xxiii, xxv,
 8–9, 13–16, 18, 28, 40, 45–49,
 51, 55, 57, 61, 64, 72, 78, 99, 101,
 112–113, 115
Mary xvii, xix, xxi, xxii, xxiii, xxiv, xxv,
 5, 8–10, 14–18, 28, 32–37, 39–40,
 42, 45–50, 52–57, 59, 61, 63–66,
 69–72, 74–75, 78–88, 90, 92–
 94, 96–103
Mary's motherhood 16, 53, 54
Mass 36, 39, 63, 71, 73, 75, 91–92
messianism 6
Messori xxiii, 3, 5, 7–8, 33, 51, 56, 85, 91–
 92, 95, 99, 102
metaphysical xix, 19–20, 25, 33–34, 38
metaphysics xix, 19, 42, 57
ministry xxiv, 28, 58, 91–93, 97–98
ministry 91, 96, 110, 115
ministry of reconciliation 93
mission xxvii, 15, 18, 28, 37, 63, 68, 69, 78,
 91–97, 101, 103, 106, 109–110
mother of Christ 16, 54, 56
Mother of God xxii, 9, 16–17, 42, 53, 55,
 86, 100
Mother of the Church xxv, 16–17, 111
Mother of the Lord 53, 86, 100, 113

motherhood 16, 17, 53–55, 57
myopic historicism 38
mystery xix, xxiv, 8, 16, 18, 21, 33, 35, 37,
       42, 47, 52, 56–59, 61, 63, 68, 72,
       77, 83, 85–86, 95, 114
Mystical Body of Christ 29, 30
Mystici Corporis 34

New Adam 42, 53, 71
New Creation 50
New Eve 42, 50, 52–53, 71
new Israel 49, 79
New Israel' 50
New Testament xxix, 9, 33, 39, 49, 67,
       112, 115

obedience 23, 71, 97
orthodoxy 20, 51, 77
orthopraxis 20, 77

pasch 88
paschal mystery 61
Patristic fidelity 15, 45
Patristic theology 21
Patristic wisdom 46
Pauline ecclesiology 33
pedagogy 72
penance 4, 5, 85
Pentecost 26, 60, 71
People of God' 30–32, 35
pilgrim People 17
pneumatological 21
post-conciliar xvii, 7–8, 46, 69, 85
Prayer 50, 70, 86–88, 92, 114
primacy 20, 22–23, 38–40, 48, 68–69, 82
Protestant Reformation 46
Protestant theology 24
Protestants 31, 99

Quasten 115
Queenship 15

Rahner, K. 113, 115
ratiocination 57
Ratzinger, J. xix, xxi, xxii, xxiii, xxiv, xxv,
       3–10, 13–42, 45–61, 63–69, 71–
       89, 91–99, 101–103, 108–109
reawakening 23
redemption 63, 90
relativism 6, 20, 102
religious 46, 56–57, 89, 93–94
Resurrection 60, 83, 89
Revelation xxvii, 19, 81, 110

sacramental 20, 37, 41, 46, 51, 61, 71,
       86, 95, 98
sacraments 59
Sacred Scriptures 110
sacrifice 60, 63–64, 66, 72, 76, 80–81,
       83–85, 89–90
Sacrosanctum Concilium xxvii, 63, 67–
       68, 70, 110
salvation xxii, xxiv, 20–21, 32, 52, 55, 60–
       61, 76, 81–82, 87, 91, 93
salvation history xxii, xxiv, 20–22,
       32, 52–53
sanctamEcclesiam 35
scepticism 6
Scholastic equation 19
Scholasticism 20
scripture 19, 33, 45, 67, 75, 80, 88, 92,
       101, 103
scriptures xxi, xxii, xxiii, xxiv, 9, 50, 52, 87
Second Vatican Council xxi, xxvii, 3, 7,
       13, 15–16, 18, 22–24, 29–30, 32,
       34, 36, 51, 60, 103, 110, 115
self-abnegation 5
self-affirmation 5, 77
self-condemnatory 4
self-gratification 77
self-immolating 93
self-revelation 20
seminal fount 5

Servant Church 93, 94
Signum Magnum 17
Societas perfecta 46
St Ambrose xxvi, 54
St Paul 29, 36–37, 41, 55, 79, 94
St Thomas Aquinas 34
St. John Paul II xix, 9
supernatural 20, 59
syncretism 10

temple 50, 63–65, 71–72, 78–81, 87, 89
Tertullian 103
The New Temple' 50
theo-drama 73, 76
theologians 7, 14, 22, 24, 30, 34, 46
theological tenets 19
theology xix, xxi, xxii, xxiii, xxiv, 5, 7, 9–
       10, 13–16, 19–20, 22, 24, 40, 47–
       48, 50, 57–58, 75, 84, 86, 93, 99
Theology xvii, xix, 3–4, 9, 15, 23, 30, 33,
       55, 68, 98, 102, 106, 108–109,
       113–115
tradition 20, 22, 23, 27, 54, 87, 88,
       100, 103
traditionalism 27
Trinity xv, 40, 67, 92, 100
triumphalism 3–4, 92–93
truth xxiii, xxiv, 3–4, 6–7, 19–20, 31, 38,
       40, 47, 51–52, 56, 58, 61, 64, 66,
       72, 77, 83, 85, 92, 97–98, 102–103,
       107, 109, 115
tyrannical secularism 6

Unity 13, 41
universal Church 22, 24, 37–42, 48, 93

Vatican xxi, xxii, xxvii, 3, 5, 7–8, 13, 15–18,
       22–24, 26–32, 34–36, 39, 41, 45,
       48, 50–51, 58, 60, 63, 67–68, 71,
       91, 93, 98–99, 103
Vatican II 106–107, 110
Verheul, A. 115
virginity 17, 88, 115
virtues 17, 32
von Balthasar xvii, 21, 26, 33, 35, 45, 48–
       49, 52–55, 57–58, 69, 73, 78–79,
       85, 94–96, 98, 105, 108, 115–116
Vorgrimler 16, 110

Wojtczak 109
Woman 17, 53, 112
Word 21, 23, 49, 53, 57, 66, 69–70, 80, 82,
       84, 87, 87, 95, 96, 100, 115
Word of God 24, 38, 54, 69, 96, 100
Worship xi, xv, xvi, xxiii, 28, 35–37, 51,
       63–68, 70, 72, 74–79, 82–86, 89

Zevini 115

Printed by
CPI books GmbH, Leck